Mullins
5822 Yarwell Drive
Houston, Texas 77096
(713) 723-6824

PATTERNS OF SUCCESS: HOW TO DISCOVER AND FOLLOW THEM

Patterns of Success: How to Discover and Follow Them

JACK FOWLER

PARKER PUBLISHING COMPANY, INC.   West Nyack, N.Y.

© 1972 *by*

PARKER PUBLISHING COMPANY, INC.

West Nyack, N.Y.

Library of Congress
Catalog Card Number: 73-172397

Printed in the United States of America
ISBN-0-13-654301-4.
B & P

How This Book Can Help You Achieve Success

If you will read this book with an open mind, without prejudice for preconceived ideas, it will be proven to you that you can be successful far beyond your dreams—and that it does not require willpower, luck, formal education, great effort, or the benevolence of other people. I will prove to you that you fail not through any lack of willpower, education or talent, but only because you have not recognized your powers—the powers you have possessed since the day you were born.

For instance, are you aware that you have within you a serving mechanism which you program with your words, thoughts, and actions? This serving mechanism is like a computer. It cannot reason—it simply performs exactly as you have programmed it. This book teaches you to recognize this serving mechanism and shows you how easily it may be programmed to respond rapidly to your instructions.

This serving mechanism always gives you results. Your instructions *have always been* carried out. However, until you learn to understand this serving mechanism and exactly how to program it, you will continue to give it instructions which create unwanted results. Most, if not all, of your failures are actually results created for you by your faithful serving mechanism through improper and uninformed instructions which you have unknowingly given it by your own words, thoughts, and actions.

For example, do you realize that the very words you speak have such power they can be singularly responsible for programming this serving mechanism to create ill health, poor memory, inability to learn and countless other harmful results? The following pages teach you a simple but exact method of using words to program your personal computer to create perfect health, social poise, a sparkling personality—whatever successes you desire. You will learn how to remove the harmful results you have created by improper programming and how to avoid giving this serving mechanism unwise instructions in the future.

Do you know that your imagination is so powerful it can and does program your serving mechanism to actually create things you fear? The following pages give you a complete understanding of how to use your imagination to overcome fears, to acquire dynamic self-confidence, and acquire new skills.

Do you know that your acting-image has such power in programming your serving mechanism as to cause it to react and adopt unwanted habits and even unwanted physical features of people with whom you identify? Again, this book teaches you how to create an acting-image and use it to program your serving mechanism to remove unwanted habits and create new and desirable ones, to improve your learning ability, or to change any aspect of your total personality you may wish to change.

Since the beginning of time man has searched for the elusive mecca "Success." Great men have devoted their lives to defining success and mapping the course to this most sought-after treasure. Millions of words have been written about success and how to attain it, and hundreds of phrases have been coined as guides to reach this golden goal: "Be Enthusiastic," "Think Positively," "The 'I Can' Attitude," "Self-Image," "Motivation," "Success Mechanism," and many, many more.

When so many great minds have searched and so many eloquent pens have written, why has the overwhelming majority of mankind failed to find success? The reasons are many, but their essence is that the majority did not answer the most important question of all: HOW to be enthusiastic, HOW to think positively, HOW to get that "I Can" attitude, HOW to change your self-image, HOW to become motivated.

The HOW is so very simple, so basic, that it does not require eloquent rhetoric, involved scientific explanations, or reams of pages to explain it to you in a manner which enables you to apply it without struggle or effort. And although the "tools of life" which are explained to you in this book have such power as to seem almost magical, there is no magic or mysticism involved. We have simply come at last to an understanding of the true nature of man and the powers he possesses.

In our past unenlightenment we have most often used these powers unknowingly to bring harm and unhappiness to ourselves. But it has now been proven that these very same tools—words, imagination, and acting-image—which have so often created unwanted results in the past can create any success you desire when you recognize their power and understand how to use them properly. Isn't it time you stopped creating failures and started creating successes which bring you personal freedom, happiness, and wealth?

In the following pages I will show you exactly HOW to recognize these powers, HOW to control them, HOW to create any success you may desire: HOW TO BE THE SUCCESSFUL INDIVIDUAL YOU WERE BORN TO BE.

Jack Fowler

Acknowledgment

*I wish to express my gratitude to Carol Webster Jochim for her
assistance, dedication, and hard work in the preparation of this book.*

Contents

PATTERNS OF SUCCESS: HOW TO DISCOVER AND FOLLOW THEM

CHAPTER ONE

Understanding the Relationship Between Success and You

What is the miracle that creates success? Many people will answer that it's simply a matter of "luck." But the variable, the determining factor between success and failure, is certainly something more tangible than the whim of "Lady Luck."

Science has proven conclusively that each of us possesses infinitely more talent than we ever use. So isn't it more logical to conclude that the degree of success we attain is determined not by how much talent we *possess*, but rather by how much of that talent *we use*?

And that question leads us to the most vital question of all. Every man wants to be successful. Why, then, do we not employ every ounce of talent we possess towards achieving success? The answer is simply that the amount of talent we expend in any area is controlled by our know-how, along with our attitude, our self-image—our beliefs. We have this talent, we just haven't recognized it or known how to use it.

Be An Individual

You are an individual, so let's consider this individuality for a moment. You were born an individual, and you will no doubt leave this plane of existence as an individual. Yet, many people never act as the individuals they are. Many act like sheep and follow the herd blindly, never even realizing that they are. You have met these people. They are grown men and women who are totally incapable of a self-determined, independent action for fear of what others may think. They never once stop to realize that these "others" are people just like themselves, all living in fear of what other people might think.

You Are Unlimited

To become a successful individual you must understand many things about yourself. You must understand how you have been conditioned in the past, what conditioned you, and how you acquired your *self-imposed* limitations. This past conditioning will be covered fully later.

But you as an individual are never limited in any way, shape, or form unless *you limit yourself.* No one else really limits you. You place these limitations on yourself if they are there—and most people do have them. You must "remove the lid," so to speak, and begin to think without limitation, way beyond what you have been thinking in the past.

Education vs. Success

Many people believe their success must necessarily be limited to the same extent their formal education or occupational training has been limited. How many times have you said or heard someone else say, "I can't make a good living because I don't have a good enough education"; "You can't get anywhere today without a college education"; "I'm just not educated enough to do that type of work or make that kind of money." Lack of education does not necessarily prevent these people from being successful—but this false belief certainly does.

Let us consider some examples of successful individuals who succeeded because they did not impose unnecessary limitations on their ability to think and act freely. One of these very successful individuals was Thomas Edison. I point him out, although he's been cited as an example many times before, to show you that he did not have—according to the standards of society—a good education. He was considered ignorant. Many people even laughed at him and ridiculed him because of his ideas. But Thomas Edison didn't stop. He believed in himself. He didn't have any doubts and he "stuck at it." The fact that people didn't understand him didn't stop him from doing what he felt he could do. He was a great man, not only for his many inventions, but because he did not waver. He stuck at it through all the rough spots. He acted on what he wanted to do.

False Beliefs Limit Your Success

There is no one who can hold back a person who believes in himself and his own talents, no matter what those talents may be. Often people come to me and say they "don't have a good enough education" to be successful. Get rid of this false belief right now. It is simply untrue.

I am aware that people are taught the importance of education through repetition and advertisements. Government publications all over the country tell people that if they do not go to college they will make so much *less* money than a college graduate. I agree that there are times when this is true—but not because of the lack of education. It is true because the person who does not go through college *believes* that he can't make as much money as the college graduate. This false belief is the main thing that keeps him from being as successful or making as much money as the college graduate.

Education—Only ONE Element of Progress

Please do not jump to the conclusion that I am belittling or minimizing the importance of formal education. One of the main purposes for our earthly existence is to learn, to progress;

to grow in our knowledge and understanding of ourselves and our fellow human beings and the world in which we live. And formal education or training is an essential element in this growth. Each of us should take advantage of every educational opportunity that is available to us.

But I am saying that education is not the *only* element of growth. If through circumstances your own education has been restricted or limited, don't be foolish enough to adopt an attitude that all progress, all growth, all success is limited. Each of us knows people who have had the benefit of an extensive formal education and who have an intelligence quotient bordering upon genius—but who are not successful financially, socially, or in any other aspect of their lives. All of us recognize that an excellent education and extraordinary intelligence do not guarantee happiness and success; so why, then, are we so eager to believe that lack of them guarantees failure?

Believe in Yourself

Most people who achieve wealth or fame were not born with it but made their own way to it. Success does not come with the speed of a flash of lightning—or even overnight. It does take time. And it is painfully obvious that the man who has a good idea but who becomes disillusioned and who loses faith in himself and his idea and gives up when success is not instantaneous, never becomes successful. Only those people who believe in something, and who make determined efforts to turn that belief into a reality, and who stick to their goal, ever achieve success.

Rely on Yourself

We do not rely on anything called "luck." Begin thinking right now that if you want something, you and you alone must achieve it. And when you want it badly enough, you will achieve it. Therefore, you will look to yourself and no one else to get what you want.

You Were BORN Successful

From the moment of birth everyone has *within himself* the ability and power to create, to achieve whatever he desires. As an infant our desires are simple and basic, just as our control over these powers is simple and basic. The natural progression would be that as we mature and develop stronger and more complex needs and desires we would also mature and develop stronger control and more versatility in using these powers. Unfortunately, due to the way we are conditioned and the way we live, we do just the opposite. We weaken our control of these God-given powers rather than strengthen and perfect it.

A child has a wonderful, vivid, creative imagination which he uses freely. As adults we stifle our imagination; we repress it; we confine it in a small mold we smugly lable "reality"; and we ridicule those whose imaginations overflow beyond the rigid bounds of this mold.

A child expresses himself and his imagination freely through the words he speaks. His words are descriptive and creative. He uses them according to an exact meaning which he understands them to have. He speaks with the conviction, simplicity, and honesty that only a child has. As adults we stifle and limit our speech. We speak in euphemisms and call it "tact." We speak disparagingly of ourselves and our abilities and call it "modesty" and "humility." We speak meaningless phrases and call it "making conversation" or "small talk." We speak without conviction or meaning.

A child believes in himself and his abilities without limitations. He has no false pride, no inhibitions, no doubts, no prejudices, and no fears of tomorrow or failure—until they are taught to him.

You may say, "Yes, but we must all grow up sometime and learn to survive in a difficult world. We can't act childish all our lives." And you equate childishness with foolishness, stupidity, naiveté, lack of responsibility.

"Tools" for Creating Success Patterns

But the point is, the creative imagination, creative wording, and absolute faith of the small child are "tools" you must learn to use to create your future successes. You were *born* successful—and you have spent the majority of your life learning *how to be unsuccessful.* The Bible tells us time and time again that we actually create with our words and our thoughts; and that when we believe without doubt, these "tools" are so powerful we can move mountains. Science has now proven conclusively that we actually do create with our words and our imagination.

Unfortunately, because we have not understood these tools and known how to use them properly, in the past we have used them primarily to create poor health, accidents, fears, and failure. Finally, however, we have learned how to control these tools, these powers, to create every right thing we desire.

No matter what you do—whether you're a carpenter or work in an office; whether you work on computers or automobiles; whether you are a dentist or a plumber; or whether you are a politician or a laborer—you can achieve greater successes each and every day of your life by using these tools properly.

The Real "You"

In the past the mind of man was believed to be divided into three sections. Freud designated these as the Id, the Ego, and the Superego—with the assumption that all three were minds.

Freud's was a good beginning; but just as time goes on and on, so does progress. And today we know that you as an individual have only one mind, and that is your conscious mind, that part of your being you refer to as "I." Your conscious mind makes decisions, makes choices, formulates desires, and can create. It's with the conscious mind that you feel your sense of identity. (See Figure 1.)

The conscious mind might be compared to the operator of a computer, with the subconscious being the computer. Your conscious mind decides what information to put into the computer, which button to push, and when to push it.

You set your goals with your conscious mind, and you use it

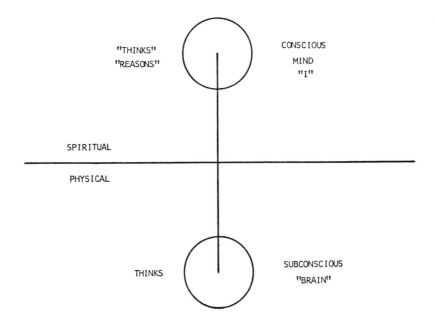

Figure 1

to gather information, make observations, evaluate incoming data and make your decisions. You have the power to reason or create with your conscious mind. An animal does not have this ability because it does not have a conscious mind.

An animal's *subconscious* can think and so can yours; but neither your subconscious nor the subconscious of animals can reason or create. Only your conscious mind has this ability. It is true that animals "create" in the sense that beavers build dams and birds build nests—but they do so instinctively and not as a result of any reasoning process. Man uses his imagination and his reasoning ability to visualize a room painted a different color, new building materials, a never-ending stream of new inventions for his comfort, convenience and productivity. But an animal, without this ability to reason, can create nothing "new" or different; and the beaver builds the same dam and the bird builds the same nest as they have through the ages.

You have the power through your conscious mind to know the difference between what is real or what is imagined; and an animal, not having a conscious mind, cannot tell the difference. You can even "make believe" with your conscious mind.

Your Subconscious

And yet you cannot materialize the slightest little thing or even make the slightest physical move with your conscious mind alone. Your subconscious must do this for you. He is a part of you, and he has specific duties to perform in addition to what your conscious mind directs him to do. The conscious mind does not entirely control the subconscious, but it can and does give it desires and goals for it to work on; and the subconscious materializes them for you.

Your subconscious will do anything for you *faster and more accurately than anything else known today*. It is actually like a computer, and it operates like a computer if you let it. It does, in other words, what you instruct or program it to do when you yourself do the programming. A major problem today is that most people do not control their own subconscious; and if you do not give your subconscious your own desires to work on, it certainly feeds on the desires of others.

You—The Master

The subconscious is a serving mechanism. Now, let me repeat this. The subconscious is a *serving mechanism*. You, as a conscious mind, may voluntarily plant in your subconscious any plan or purpose which you want it to work on, which you desire to be translated into the physical or material, and the subconscious will react accordingly.

Your subconscious is never idle. It is constantly in need of nourishment, things to do. If you fail to feed your subconscious your desires, it feeds upon either the desires of others or random thoughts that reach it. In other words, *your conscious mind must be the controlling factor*, the master of your subconscious. You must give your subconscious your desires to work on at all times or it will function as a slave to the desires of others and really master you.

And remember, your subconscious cannot reason. Therefore, it cannot tell the difference between a real experience and one that you imagine. What you imagine in your conscious mind in vivid detail is, to your subconscious, *the same thing as a real experience.*

A Contradiction

Your subconscious functions voluntarily whether you make any effort to influence it or not; for it does think by itself. It thinks *independently* of your conscious mind; sometimes in agreement with it, and *sometimes in direct contradiction to it.*

Now, this is very important for you to understand. The conscious mind thinks for itself; the subconscious thinks for itself. But the conscious mind can reason (or create); whereas the subconscious cannot.

So now there are actually two basic parts of you thinking, either separately or together, aren't there? The big difference is that the subconscious cannot reason or create like the conscious mind. Bu the subconscious does think for itself; and many times it reacts according to what it does think.

Conflicts in Thinking

If the subconscious and the conscious mind do not work together, trouble is sure to follow. The biggest single problem in the world today is that most people allow their subconscious to control them. They are actually, as a conscious mind, reacting to the desires and whims of the subconscious; and this is not the way it should be. Your subconscious can and must be controlled by your conscious mind.

Your subconscious may still be reacting to something you once believed. Therefore, today you may have difficulty in responding to a newly acquired belief. This conflict between the belief to which your subconscious is still responding and the belief newly acquired by your conscious mind can cause serious problems. You may be completely unaware of this previous conditioning. And even if you are aware of it, you still might not understand it.

The subconscious reacts in the manner in which it has been conditioned to react, mainly because you conditioned it to accept certain things as fact. When the subconscious continues to react to something that happened years ago or some suggestion given to it a long time ago which you no longer recall, this, of course, can create a problem. And today your conscious mind doesn't really understand or know why you can't do a particular thing or break some habit. This disagreement or conflict between the conscious mind and the subconscious is the major cause of mental sickness.

A New Acquaintance

If you're like most people, in the past your subconscious really hasn't done the things you wanted it to do because you have not been in ideal communication with it. There have been many reasons for this poor communication with your subconscious, but I'm going to open the door for you to get better acquainted with it.

The subconscious has not been taken into consideration in the teachings you have received or in the way you have been conditioned in the past. Very little has been known and understood about the subconscious until recent years. Unfortunately, what was known wasn't fully believed and accepted until more scientific facts were brought out. The result of this earlier lack of knowledge has been that during your lifetime you have actually conditioned your subconscious to pay little attention to you. Your subconscious was designed to be your servant, but you have conditioned it not to listen to you at all.

Don't Cry Wolf

Remember the story about the little boy who cried wolf? He

would go into the hills to play; and he soon discovered that he could scream and cry "wolf" and all the townspeople would rush to his aid—believing, of course, that a wolf was after the little boy—only to find there wasn't any wolf at all. The little boy got a big kick out of seeing all those people running to help him.

After having done this a considerable number of times, one day the little boy went into the hills again to play, only this time a real wolf was after him. He screamed and cried "wolf" again, but not one single person paid any attention to him. They thought he was up to his old tricks again and they completely ignored him.

Well, your subconscious is like the people in this story; and your conscious mind is like the little boy. When the conscious mind "cries wolf" too many times, the subconscious just doesn't pay any attention to it. Your subconscious cannot reason with your thoughts or statements. It takes your words literally until you cry wolf too many times; then it simply ignores them completely because you have conditioned it to do just that.

You must understand that you are also retraining your conscious mind. In the past your subconscious has run the show in any "hit or miss" fashion because you have not given it direction. You have not controlled it in any way. Now you are beginning to do so.

IMPORTANT POINTS TO RECALL

1. You were born successful.
2. Science has proven that you presently use only a small portion of your talents.
3. The amount of your talent you use is determined by your past conditioning.
4. Any limitations on your success are self-imposed, placed there by your past conditioning.
5. Limited education does not necessarily mean limited success.
6. You can, and do, create with your words and thoughts.

7. Every tool, every power needed to be successful, is right within you *now*.
8. You alone control your future, your successes.
9. You have only one "mind"—your conscious mind.
10. Your conscious mind—

    Is the real you; makes decisions and formulates desires; can think and reason; must master and control your subconscious.

11. Your subconscious—

    Cannot reason and therefore cannot tell the difference between a real experience and one which is imagined in vivid detail; materializes your desires; can think—and does so independently of the conscious mind and sometimes in direct contradiction to the conscious mind.

CHAPTER TWO

How to
Discover the Real You

Now that you have a better understanding of how the conscious mind and the subconscious function, how they relate to each other, and what the proper duties of each of them are, you should now proceed to learn more about how you have been conditioned in the past and what conditioned you.

Most people never realize *why* they think and act as they do. They don't know how or why they acquired their present beliefs and attitudes—the hopes, fears, preferences, prejudices, ambitions and desires which comprise the particular personality they are. It is absolutely necessary for you to know what your present beliefs are and know and understand the influences which created them, because these very same influences and "tools" which have molded and forged the present "you" are the very things you will use to create your happy, successful future. You will be taught to recognize all these tools and shown HOW to use them properly.

You use these "tools," as I call them, each and every day of your life. You should learn to understand them and recognize their true value. You must know that these tools are indeed very effective. You must also know that you are either using these tools or they are using you. It is always one way or the other.

Master or Slave

When you begin to see how you have been controlled by these tools in the past, you will know without doubt that these tools are indeed very powerful and you will use them to create a planned, successful future. You will be the master, and no longer a slave to unknown conditioning.

Past Conditioning

Let's proceed to discuss some of the basic influences which created your present beliefs and attitudes, the personality that is the present "you." We could spend many hours just discussing past conditioning alone; but the available space and time dictate that I give you just those essential details which enable you to understand these tools clearly and develop absolute faith in their effectiveness, their tremendous power.

Basic Causes of a Neurosis

If you were to become a psychotherapist, you would learn what causes people to have what we call "mental sickness." In the field of psychotherapy the basic causes of mental sickness have been broken down into categories. Some of the most frequently encountered basic causes of a neurosis are: effect of suggestion, creative wording, creative imagination, identification, past experiences, and conflict.

It is very important for you to understand that everyone could undergo psychotherapy to better his understanding of himself and to create a happier, more well-adjusted life. You should understand these basic causes of mental sickness and know how you may have been affected by them in the past. Then you must learn how you can use these very same basic causes of a neurosis to better your future, so you can become the master of your future and no longer be the slave of these conditionings.

Effect of Suggestion—or Power of Suggestion

The "power of suggestion" is a term with which you are probably familiar. In basic psychology there is a term called "effect of suggestion" which is really the same thing as the "power of suggestion" except that it implies that you have been *affected* by a certain suggestion.

Everyone is subject to the effect of suggestion. Simply defined, it means what you believe from what your senses tell you. Everything that you see, hear, touch, taste, or smell is observed and recorded by your subconscious. You pay little or no attention to some of these things with your conscious mind. And even though you are aware of some of them, you do not usually recognize their effect or power upon you.

Varying Degrees of Susceptibility

Everyone is suggestible to some extent or it would be impossible for us to learn new things; but not everyone is suggestible to the same degree. Do not confuse suggestibility with gullibility. They are two entirely different matters.

Your degree of suggestibility largely determines your degree of susceptibility to hypnosis; and when working with hypnosis you soon discover that some people are very susceptible while others are susceptible only to a minor degree. I think everyone will agree that children are suggestible to the greatest degree. And yet this vulnerability to suggestion is often overlooked and they are subjected to adverse suggestions that do them great harm.

Understanding Effect of Suggestion

Your degree of susceptibility to suggestion is something that you must learn about yourself. This suggestibility can be either good for you or very bad for you, depending upon the judgment and selectivity you exercise in deciding which suggestions to accept and which to reject.

It's important to determine your degree of response to suggestion for two main reasons. First, and most important, is that if you do not know your degree of response to suggestion, you are not aware of the effect of suggestion, or the power of suggestion, upon you. There will continue to be a probability that you will accept suggestions which are harmful to you and limit your success. You may not even be consciously aware that a suggestion has been accepted and is being reacted to by your subconscious; and this certainly can create problems for you and can defeat you in any progress you desire.

Second, when you understand the effect of suggestion and your susceptibility to it, you can make suggestion work for you. It is an effective tool at your command.

Suggestions Come from Many Sources

We are often affected by the suggestions of persons in authority, people in the entertainment world or others in the public eye, and those people who gain our respect and admiration. We look up to them and we respect what they say.

Doctors are well-respected and justly so for they do much good in the world. People generally believe what doctors say to be absolute fact. For this reason they must be extremely careful of what they do say—and even more so to children or around children. A parent, a doctor—and even a public official—is in a good position to make effective use of suggestions. Many people believe what is said by a public figure, even when they know practically nothing about the person involved or the subject about which he is speaking.

Repetition Reinforces Effect of Suggestion

Repetition is one of the best ways of making suggestion effective. As children we are frequently told the same thing again and again as a means of teaching us or training us until an indelible imprint is left on our subconscious.

Advertising is perhaps the largest single planned form of suggestion we know today; and advertisers keep pouring millions and millions of dollars behind repetition. Religion is a form of suggestion, too.

Using Your Power of Choice

Your subconscious always responds to words or suggestions which you accept to be true; and your subconscious accepts them literally, word for word, because it cannot do anything other than that—it cannot reason.

You're an intelligent adult now, capable of determining what is best for you. You can keep undesirable suggestions from being put into your subconscious by rejecting them with your conscious mind. As an adult you've learned to reason with your conscious mind and you have better judgment to accept or reject information that is presented to you. You can sift it for facts and weigh information for truths and feed to your subconscious as fact only what you choose to accept.

Creative Wording

Creative wording is another important basic cause of a neurosis. It is also one of the major tools you will learn to use to create that new, successful "you" that you long to be.

Creative wording is such a vital tool in controlling your subconscious and in learning to master yourself and your future that an entire chapter is devoted to creative wording later in the book. But at this time it is essential that you understand the meaning of creative wording and know the tremendous power it has so you can understand the part it has played in your past conditioning and know just how strongly you have been affected by it.

Simply stated, when I speak of creative wording I am talking about words and their effect upon you. Again, your subconscious cannot reason with words as your conscious mind does, and it takes your words literally, word for word. Your subconscious responds to your words and sometimes translates them into an actual physical condition—especially when they are repeated over and over again for some time.

Only *creative* wording brings about this end result; and the end result can be good or bad, depending on how this powerful tool is used. In learning about creative wording—how it has affected you in the past and how to use it properly in creating the future you desire—there are several points which must be thoroughly understood.

Your Words *Do* Create an End Result

First, it has been scientifically proven that the words we speak do have power; and when they are used as creative wording, they do create an end result because they motivate your subconscious to react and materialize exactly what the words say.

Can you begin to fathom the fantastic power that is available to you knowing that words have the power to create and that you can learn to use them properly to create exactly what you desire? According to Webster, "creative" means: "Having the power or quality of creating." And "to create" means: "To bring into being; to cause to exist . . . To produce, form or bring to pass . . . as a work of thought or imagination." And this expresses exactly what you wish to accomplish.

Creative wording does have the power of creating. It has played an important role in investing you with the character, the personality that is the present "you" and it will play a major role in creating the new, successful "you."

Creative Wording Defined

Secondly, you must understand exactly what creative wording is. Creative wording is any phrase, statement, or series of words which explicitly expresses a presence, a condition, or a state of being as existing HERE AND NOW.

Let me give you some examples of creative wording and non-creative wording which will help you to understand this definition. For instance, you may have a strong desire to learn to play the piano. Because your subconscious is a goal-striving mechanism which you can control or program by words and thoughts which are used repetitively, you know that through your words you can convey this desire, this goal, to your subconscious and it will materialize this goal for you. The big question is, what words do you use to convey this goal properly to your subconscious so it will react to them?

Here and Now

Let me repeat our definition of creative wording: creative wording is any phrase, statement, or series of words which explicitly expresses a presence, a condition, or a state of being as existing *here and now*. Since it must be expressed as existing here and now, you don't use words such as "I am going to," "I will," "I'll try," etc., because these words are not definite as to time. They do not mean "here and now," but only that at some nebulous time in the future you "may be." These phrases also imply doubt. Therefore, even if a time limit is stated, your subconscious will not accept them as expressing a sincere desire and it will not react to them.

You Must Be Explicit

If you say, "I play well," that does express a condition as existing here and now—but it is not explicit as to *what* condition. What do you play well? Golf, poker, the harp?

The proper creative wording you would use to convey this goal to your subconscious is, "I play the piano well." Analyze this statement for a moment: "I play the piano well." It is explicit; it expresses a condition or a state of being; and it expresses that condition as existing here and now. Therefore, it is proper creative wording. And if it is repeated frequently enough over a long enough period of time, your subconscious will accept it as your true, sincere desire, and it will react to this desire and materialize it for you—and you will play the piano well.

Because creative wording has never been defined for you before and is a totally new concept, you may not understand it fully until you have read further in this chapter or until you complete the chapter "Using Your Voice to Create Success." But as you read on, the meaning, the proper usage, and the unlimited power of creative wording will be made abundantly clear to you.

Both Good and Bad Results

The third point you must understand about creative wording—and it is an extremely important point—is that creative wording can create bad results as well as good results. Unfortunately, because it has not been understood before, in the past it has most frequently been used to create *bad* results. Remember that creative wording is *any* phrase, statement, or series of words which explicitly expresses a presence, a condition, or a state of being as existing here and now. Therefore, if you say, "I can't remember," this statement fulfills all the requirements of creative wording. It *is* creative wording, and through repetition your subconscious will react to it and you will actually have poor memory recall. You will have created a bad result.

When you say, "Coffee always keeps me awake at night," again through repetition your subconscious accepts this as your sincere desire; and it then reacts to it and does indeed keep you awake at night. Another bad result.

So you see, creative wording creates either good or bad results, depending on how you use it. You should begin right now to be aware of the power of the words you speak and use them to create *only what you want*. Some of these points may be a little difficult for you to understand clearly in the beginning, but as you read on you will gain a thorough understanding of them and you can begin to use creative wording to create only those things which you desire.

"That Gives Me a Headache"

The following case history demonstrates the use of creative wording to achieve a very bad result. This patient had been going to a doctor for treatment for headaches. The doctor prescribed many drugs for relief of the pain, but as time went on the drugs were completely ineffective in relieving his discomfort. Finally the man was referred to my office for treatment to uncover the *cause* of his headaches.

During the first hour of treatment this man repeatedly made statements that this or that "gives me a headache." He must have repeated statements such as: "Oh, he gives me a headache"; "She gives me a headache"; "That really gives me a headache," etc., a few dozen times during that first hour. You can see that this man was using creative wording. Creative wording does create an end result from what the individual says over and over again; and in this case it created a headache for this man. His headaches were caused only by repeated statements that this or that "gives me a headache."

It was discovered that this man had used such statements for well over seven years. I explained creative wording to him and showed him what he was doing to himself. Once he understood this, of course he made a change in his habit of speech. In order to help him, I made up some three-by-five cards; and every time he caught himself saying that something gives him a headache he was to read the cards. The cards were very effective and he soon changed his habit of speech. He began to adopt new phrases which he could repeat to himself as often as he wanted because this new creative wording was good for him. He began saying things like: "He makes me feel wonderful." "She makes me feel marvelous." "That makes me feel great," and so on. Within a few weeks his headaches were gone completely; and when I saw him a few months later he said he hadn't had a headache since.

This man had actually been forcing his subconscious to work against him. He didn't know it, of course. When creative wording was explained to him he soon realized that to repeat these statements could bring him harm and they actually did create the end result. He also knew now that he could get his subconscious to do anything he wanted it to do by using creative wording.

The Key Is Repetition

The key to this power of creative wording is repetition, developing a habit of speech by repeating the same words over and over again for many days or months, and years if necessary. Repetition is one of the major basic tools you are learning to use to create your successful future; and it is used in conjunction with the three other major tools: creative wording, creative imagination, and acting-image.

When learning to type or drive a car the same thing has to be repeated again and again many times before your subconscious takes over and does it for you. The same thing applies with creative wording. By repeating words over and over again, your subconscious will take over and create what is being said by the words—not what you intend, but what the words actually say, because your subconscious cannot reason and reacts to its literal understanding of the words. You then get an end result.

One of the many things the Bible tells us about is the power of words. "By thy words thou shall be justified and by thy words thou shall be condemned." So take heed when you learn about words. And the key to this power, as I said before, is repetition: repeating the same statement over and over again, developing a habit by repeating the words many times every day.

"That Gets Under My Skin"

Let me give you another case history to demonstrate the power of words because this power is very, very important. This particular man had a terrible skin disease all over his body. In this case, this man constantly repeated such statements as: "He gets under my skin." "She gets under my skin." "That really gets under my skin," and so on.

This man was also told about creative wording and how it affects people who use it over a long period of time. He was taught to use different words, words that would give him an end result that he wanted. Within a month his skin was completely cleared up.

This sounds a little fantastic, doesn't it? But *the power of words is fantastic;* and this type of reaction to words occurs much more commonly than you think. I find that everyone I meet uses such terminology in his speech. If you consistently use such ill-chosen statements as a habit of speech—or in your thoughts, even—you are in danger of allowing such conditions to occur.

Harmful Creative Wording in Common Usage

There are many, many examples of harmful creative wording which are in such common usage people overlook them—and unfortunately, they use them as habits of speech. Which of the following expressions is used as a habit of speech either by yourself or others you come in contact with?

I can't see that.	That gives me a headache.
I'll be damned.	It makes me sick at my stomach.
I can't stand it.	It's a pain in the neck to me.
That slays me.	He gets under my skin.
That makes me ill.	That really gives me a pain.
I can't stand him.	He makes me sick.
That makes me sore.	That sure burns me up.
I can't stomach that.	Boy, that really kills me.
I can't swallow that.	He drives me crazy.

Find some other examples for yourself. You use creative wording in some way. Find out what it is and what it has created for you. You will soon prove to yourself, beyond any doubt, the power of creative wording and what it has done and can do for you, either good or bad.

Let's scrutinize just a few more examples of creative wording and understand what they really do say. You might be discussing an idea with which you disagree and you may comment, "I can't see that." Now, you are really disagreeing with the idea, aren't you? But that isn't what you're *saying*. When you were in school you learned the actual meaning of words, word by word; and when you say, "I can't *see*," you're talking about "eyesight" to your subconscious, aren't you? Remember: your subconscious cannot reason; so he accepts the words literally, word for word. If you use this expression as a habit of speech, you are in grave danger of acquiring poor eyesight.

What about the person who continually says, "I'll be damned"? This person is in jeopardy of becoming accident-prone. And many people have a habit of saying, "I can't stand him," or "I can't stand her," or "I can't stand that." These people are in peril of having back trouble or leg trouble, or any problem of such a nature that they cannot *stand*. When you speak a creatively worded statement, your subconscious is being conditioned to respond to what you *say*, not what you *think*, especially when you use repetition.

Everyone Is Susceptible

Do not believe that every time you use a statement such as the examples given that you will develop the end result. The key to creative wording is repetition. Some people may be able to implant an idea in their subconscious in six months, others may take six years; and some may take only six weeks.

There are no exceptions, though. Everyone is susceptible and will respond to some degree—some to a lesser and some to a greater degree—depending, of course, on the individual.

Beginning right now, be aware of the words you use. Examine what you say and all that is said within your hearing. Be aware at all times what is happening to you and what you are doing to yourself. Remove the blocks caused by bad creative wording and replace them with words which create good results instead of bad. You'll discover from this moment on you are well aware of the harmful phrases you yourself use. You'll catch yourself saying them and begin correcting them.

Creative Imagination

Creative imagination is another of the basic causes of neuroses and is also a major tool or power to be used in creating your future successes. Creative imagination is discussed in depth in a later chapter, but again it is necessary for you to understand it at this time so you may know the role it has played in your past conditioning and the creation of the present "you."

There is a difference between "imagination" and *"creative* imagination." In order to use creative imagination, you must do the creating in your conscious mind; and your subconscious will materialize what your conscious mind creates.

Let's approach creative imagination by analyzing and understanding fear and how fear conditions you, since fear is nothing but imagination. Foolish fears are an example of how you let your imagination use you instead of your using it. And it is true, of course, that people basically let imagination use them instead of their using imagination to create what they want.

Imagination Effects a "Cure"

Dr. Robert Smith, an eye, ear, nose and throat specialist, once told me of how imagination contributes to the symptoms complained of by some of his patients and how he makes use of this tool in his treatment of these people.

Because of the nature of Dr. Smith's specialty, many people come to him for throat ailments. In some instances no physical reason can be found for their discomfort. In the early years of his practice, after having examined a patient and having found no physical condition which would cause the symptoms complained of, Dr. Smith would simply tell the patient that he could find no problem and that the patient had presumably just scratched his throat and caused a little irritation which would soon disappear. But these patients would come back time and time again complaining of soreness or something "stuck" in their throat.

During the years of his practice, Dr. Smith discovered that many times—if there was no physical explanation to be found through careful testing and diagnosis—the symptoms could be cured by using the power of the patient's imagination and may even, at times, have been created in the patient's imagination. Dr. Smith devised a very simple but effective procedure which he used when he believed imagination was the true culprit in creating the patient's discomfort or could be employed to relieve it. While examining the patient's throat, the doctor would pretend to "extract" a small particle from it. He would tell the patient he had found the cause of the irritation and had removed it, and that in a day or two the irritation would be completely gone and he would have no further trouble. Even though the particle the doctor removed was only imaginary, or perhaps some small fragment which the doctor himself had placed in the instrument to show to the patient, these patients *believed* the cause of their problem had been removed. And the irritation and discomfort did indeed disappear in a day or two and the patients had no further symptoms.

Regardless of whether the problem the patient was having was created by a true physical condition or whether it was created by his imagination, the only thing used in effecting a "cure" was the patient's own imagination. He *imagined* that the doctor had actually removed an irritant from his throat and that the reason for his discomfort was no longer present—and the discomfort disappeared.

Fear Is a Form of Creative Imagination

I would like to give you a case history which illustrates the use of creative imagination in the form of fear to create a very serious and harmful result. This is the case of a man who was sent to me for counselling because he had a serious skin problem that would not respond to any type of medical treatment. His skin would puff up into blisters which would break and bleed; and medication had no effect at all.

This man was put into deep hypnosis and regressed back to the time of his childhood. It was discovered that at the age of three he was taught to fear the dark with repeated warnings that "the bogeyman is going to get you."

Then at the age of five he had an experience which later caused his skin problem. He was locked into a pitch-dark basement where he knew that spiders and insects existed. The basement was all dirt, with no concrete on the floor or walls. With his tremendous fear of the dark, he felt sure that this "bogeyman" was going to grab him while he was locked in this dark basement. He imagined the "bogeyman" was grabbing him, touching his skin. And he imagined that all those insects and bugs were crawling all over his skin. While under hypnosis he recalled his feelings at that time; and later he made the statement, "I wasn't afraid; I was petrified!"

This man actually had two neuroses. The first one, his fear of the dark, was acquired at the age of three. Then the experience he had in the dark basement at the age of five when he imagined the "bogeyman" was grabbing him and imagined that the bugs and insects were crawling on his skin was so traumatic for him that it also created a neurosis. The first neurosis was dominating and until it was removed the second neurosis remained in the background, buried in his subconscious. But when this first neurosis was "cured" or when the fear of the darkness left him at the age of 25, the second neurosis, created by his experience in the basement, expressed itself through the skin eruptions which first occurred at the age of 25.

Once this man understood this completely, his skin immediately began to clear up. Within four weeks all the blisters and eruptions were gone and he had no signs of a skin problem.

Fear Is Easily Instilled in Children

Of course, it is easy to instill fear in a child because a child doesn't have the knowledge and training, the reasoning ability that an adult has. We know this. That's why children are more susceptible to suggestions and ideas; and that's why in psychotherapy we generally look into a person's childhood or formative years for the root of most problems.

Don't Create Fears About Tomorrow

We are told in the Bible, "Take no thought for the morrow," and we should follow this admonition. But most people are always worrying about tomorrow. They think about what might happen or what they *imagine* will happen, and they dwell on these things until, through wrongfully applying their creative imagination, they actually create fear. Creative imagination is the culprit, but only when you misuse it, because *you* create the thoughts; and the thoughts must be created to get an end result—even a bad result.

Permit me to add here to what the Bible said about words and let me say, "By thy *imagination* thou shall be justified and by thy *imagination* thou shall be condemned." When used correctly, imagination is a very powerful tool which you have at your command. When used incorrectly, it is a very destructive tool which you frequently use against yourself.

Use Vivid Detail

You can easily see how imagination can hold a person back. Is there any doubt about its power? Stop for a few minutes and give thought to how wonderful life could be if you didn't let imagination use you, if you didn't fear anything. Imagination, this same powerful tool that creates problems, can be used to create successes.

We can understand creative imagination and what causes it to work by understanding a little more about fear and how it works. These fears you imagine are in vivid detail; and because your subconscious cannot reason or tell the difference between reality and what is imagined in vivid detail, your subconscious accepts these fears as fact and reacts accordingly to materialize the end result. In order to use your imagination for what you want, you can and must create these desires in your imagination in just as vivid detail as you create the fears that harm you and hold you back.

I will take a moment here to show you just how much detail is available to you in creating fears or in creating your goals in your imagination. You must realize that every sense impression is recorded by your subconscious even when you are not consciously aware of the impression. For example, when someone comes to my office for counselling I may ask him to describe in detail the trip he has just completed between his home or office and my office. Generally he will give a very brief, vague description summed up with the comment that he "really wasn't paying that much attention, his mind was occupied elsewhere. He was thinking about other things and just didn't notice much about the trip."

But when this same person is put into deep hypnosis and asked to relate to me all the details of his trip to my office, he describes hundreds upon hundreds of details of which he was not consciously aware but which his subconscious recorded during the trip. In fact, if I permitted him to continue until he had actually related every detail his subconscious recorded during his trip to my office, it would take many hours for such a lengthy recitation. He could recall and relate every sight, sound or smell that was within his range of observation during the entire trip, though consciously he might be willing to swear that he had observed only a very minute fraction of them.

I believe you can begin to envision the unending detail which is recorded in your subconscious, the detail which your subconscious has stored and which is used when you give your imagination free reign to create fears rather than controlling it and using it to create your desires. You can now understand why fear, imagined in such vivid detail, actually creates an end result more rapidly than you achieve your goals by using this same tool. Generally when you use your imagination to create a mental picture of your goal you overlook many of these small details.

It is important that you understand and remember that you must picture your goal in as vivid detail as possible when using your creative imagination. The more absolute and vivid the detail you use in creating this mental picture in your imagination, the more powerful this tool of creative imagination becomes and the more rapidly you achieve your goals.

Repetition

Do not overlook repetition. We have already discussed repetition many times, but it is absolutely essential that you understand how very important this basic tool is. These mental pictures which you create over and over again are the ones which cause your subconscious to make them real or to materialize them for you. As I said earlier, your subconscious does not know the difference between a real experience and an imagined experience; so if you imagine a successful experience in vivid detail, your subconscious is being conditioned to that successful experience.

Identification

As young children we all tend to identify with movie stars, parents, an aunt or uncle, an older cousin. We may even identify with an older brother, sister or friend. However, because it is a normal desire in any child to be strong and independent and able to do as he pleases, he will most often identify with adults who appear to him to have this power and freedom.

Children do not identify only with those they love. A child may feel hatred for a parent or older brother or sister but have a strong desire to be like that hated person who has the power to tell him what he can or cannot do, the power to have his own way or to mete out punishment.

As adults we often contribute to a child's identification with another person by repeatedly telling the child, "You are the spitting image of your mother," "You certainly have your father's disposition," or "You are stubborn, just like your Uncle Charles." And particularly if the child already identifies with that person, you enhance his tendency to imitate his "father's disposition," or "Uncle Charles' stubbornness."

Imitation—Both Conscious and Unconscious

When we identify with another person, we dramatize, we

imitate that person. We usually do this consciously, but we are developing a habit *unconsciously*.

A child may unconsciously imitate physical attributes as well as personality characteristics and traits. If a parent has an uncontrolled temper, the child who identifies with the parent may display more temper as a means of imitation. If the person with whom the child identifies is overweight, the child may become overweight in order to become more like that person.

Why You Identify with Other People

The pertinent question here is, "Why do we identify with other people?" And the answer is that we identify with people we admire or people we *want to be like*. We identify with someone because he has a pleasing personality and everybody likes him or because he is respected owing to his power or position, such as a king or queen, a world leader, or some other public figure. We want to be able to evoke the same love, admiration and respect, and possess the same power and authority, as these people we identify with and imitate.

We consciously identify only with the personalities of these people and the love, admiration, respect and power they garner from others. But subconsciously we adopt or accept other characteristics connected with these people such as their physical appearance, their mannerisms, and their habits.

Identification Is Not Limited to Children

Children certainly have no monopoly on identification. How many of us imitate entertainment personalities or public figures in our manner of dress, our hairstyles, our bearing, our habits of speech, and countless other ways? How many thousands of women imitated the Jackie Kennedy or Barbra Streisand hairdo, the Twiggy makeup, the Bonnie and Clyde clothes styles? How many thousands of men imitated the Beatles' long hair and "mod" style of dress? We imitate the moral code, the political convictions, the personal ethics of these people with whom we identify. We even try to make our own physical proportions conform to those of the people we liken ourselves to.

Identification can benefit us if we identify with those people vho are truly worthy of emulation and imitate those attributes which are admirable. If you admire someone who has a radiant, magnetic personality, it is well to imitate that person to the extent that you also develop your own radiant, magnetic personality—but *only* the personality, not the other aspects of that person's habits or physical appearance.

Past Experiences

We are all largely the product of our past experiences and the way we have been conditioned by them. Mental illness is almost always rooted in some occurrence in our past. These incidents need not necessarily be major events in our lives, but something about the particular experience was traumatic to us and implanted itself in our subconscious as a basis of a neurosis. We may consciously or unconsciously have guilt feelings about a past experience.

Although we may not recall these experiences or be aware of any significance or importance attached to them, we may still be reacting to them and are limited and controlled to varying degrees by them. The young man who was locked in the basement and imagined the "bogeyman" was grabbing him and the bugs and insects were crawling on his skin had no conscious recollection of his incident. Still, the experience left a deep impression on his subconscious; and his subconscious continued to react to it with tragic results.

Fear of Spending

Past experiences are the root of many fears we have today. Perhaps as a child a person experienced poverty and deprivation. Even though circumstances have changed tremendously and his present income is more than adequate to provide comfort or even luxury, he may have a fear of spending money.

It might well be that an attitude towards spending money which is more in keeping with his present financial situation would be greatly beneficial to him. Better clothing might enable him to make a better appearance and thereby lead to a promotion in his job. The purchase of a new car might mean an ultimate financial savings as opposed to continual repairs on the old one. A business expansion might return many times the cost required for the expansion. But because he is still responding to the poverty he experienced as a child and the need for frugality at that time, this man is literally *unable* to spend money even for self-advancement or to take advantage of opportunities for his own gain.

Fear of Hunger

Perhaps the most painful part of the poverty this man experienced as a child, and the part which left the deepest impression on him, was hunger. Even though conditions today are such that food is plentiful, he may still be reacting to that experience when every scrap of food he could find was not enough to assuage his hunger—and he may be a compulsive eater, even to the point of gluttony.

Fear of Rejection

If as a child you were ungainly and awkward, perhaps considered "plain," or some aspect of your physical appearance was a target for ridicule by the other children, this experience would be painful to you, of course. You would feel rejected and insecure in the company of other people.

Today you may be a very handsome man or a beautiful woman in whose company anyone would find pleasure. But because you have not re-appraised your self-image, you still react to this painful childhood experience. You subconsciously fear rejection, and you are withdrawn, afraid to make friendly overtures to people, afraid to meet new people.

Fear of Failure

Or as a child you may have failed at something and been subjected to embarrassment and ridicule for your failure. Your self-confidence was undermined to the point where you developed a pattern of failure.

Today you may well have the intelligence, the talent, every ability to be an outstanding example of a successful individual. But again you have not re-evaluated your self-image. You still avoid new ventures, new endeavors in which your abilities have not been tried and proven because you fear you will fail and suffer ridicule.

Look at Your Own Fears

There are countless fears which you create in your own mind. Most of them are unrealistic and most of them stem from past experiences that are unrelated to your present circumstances, but you still allow them to influence you and even control you.

Take a realistic and critical look at your own fears. Determine the basis for the fear. Most often you will find that the fear stemmed from some past experience and is completely unfounded, or even absurd, in light of your present abilities and circumstances.

Conflicts

As you learned earlier, only your conscious mind has the ability to reason. But both your conscious mind and the subconscious have the ability to think—and sometimes they think in agreement with each other and sometimes in direct contradiction to each other. This disparity between the thinking of the conscious mind and the thinking of the subconscious results in a conflict between those two elements of your total self. This conflict has a tremendously strong effect upon you. It is a basic cause of a neurosis and can often lead to serious mental illness.

Conflicts between your conscious mind and your subconscious can cause frustration and a feeling of futility. They can make you impotent in your efforts to change an unwanted habit. They can instill an unrealistic sense of guilt within you or rob you of self-confidence. They color your self-image and your acting-image. And they most definitely limit any successes you may attain.

Because these conflicts can have such a far-reaching effect upon you and your life, it is of the utmost importance that you understand how such conflicts arise. You must be aware of the influence they bring to bear on your attitudes, beliefs, self-image and acting-image. And you must learn to resolve and eliminate these conflicts.

As you now know, everyone is susceptible to suggestion to some degree; and suggestions are received from many sources through our five senses. If you are not aware of the power of suggestion, a suggestion may be accepted by your subconscious without your consciously being aware of it. If you later accept a fact with your conscious mind which is contradictory to the fact already accepted by your subconscious, you then have a conflict between the thinking of your conscious mind and the subconscious.

How Conflicts Begin

Let's examine for a moment how a conflict might arise and what problems it may cause. Let's suppose an infant is born into a family which is very devout in a particular faith, and the baby is baptized into that church. The infant's family is very faithful in their attendance at all church services and in their adherence to all the teachings of that religion.

The baby, of course, is too young to understand these religious teachings; but his subconscious records everything, even from the time of birth. His subconscious records everything from the church meetings he is taken to by his parents, and it records everything said and done by the family or anyone else within his range of observation. We must recognize that an infant or small child is not consciously educated enough to accept or reject suggestions, and his subconscious records everything and "thinks" according to these suggestions it receives. So this baby constantly accepts the suggestions he receives about this particular religion and the thinking of his subconscious is patterned according to these suggestions.

Then perhaps when the child is seven or eight years old the parents undergo a change in their beliefs and thinking and they convert to a different religious thought or concept, different religious teachings; and from that point on the child is raised according to this new faith or belief of his parents.

As the child grows up he may not even recall or be aware that his very first religious teachings were contrary to those he received from the age of seven or eight on. He is consciously unaware of all the suggestions his subconscious accepted relating to the original teachings he received. Therefore, as he grows up in this new church he may commit "sins" against the religion into which he was born and first baptized. He will have a conflict because he is unaware of the teachings of the first religion and cannot consciously accept or reject them.

Perhaps according to the doctrine of the first religion it was a sin to play cards, to attend movies or dances, and to smoke or drink. Since he does not recall the particular teachings he received and these activities are not contrary to his present *conscious* religious beliefs, he may sometimes go to movies and dances, he may smoke or drink, or he may enjoy an occasional game of cards. When he does these things he is committing a sin according to the thinking of his subconscious because it still thinks in accordance with the teachings of the first religion. This man now has a conflict between the thinking of his conscious mind and his subconscious. He has a neurosis.

Everyone Has Conflicts

This is just one very obvious example of how conflicts may

arise between the thinking of the conscious mind and the subconscious. All of us have conflicts arising from suggestions. These may be suggestions we accepted without even being aware of them, or suggestions we cannot recall. Or a conflict can occur when we change the thinking of our conscious mind without also changing the thinking of our subconscious.

You Are a Product of Past Conditioning

I have now touched upon some of the recognized basic causes of a neurosis. My discussion of them has necessarily been brief, but I believe it has been sufficient to make you aware that you are, in a very large part, the product of your past conditioning. This conditioning and the way you have reacted to it—and are still reacting to it—has created your present personality, your attitude, your self-image—or, to sum up, your beliefs.

You should also be aware by now that many of your beliefs are inconsistent with the reality of now. They are based on situations or circumstances which no longer exist, falsehoods which you were too young or too immature to reject, experiences which left fears because you could not rationalize them or understand them as a child. You now have the maturity and the wisdom to discard and remove any influence, limitation, or control which these false beliefs have placed upon you.

> "The greatest discovery of my generation is that human beings can alter their lives by altering their attitudes of mind."
>
> William James

False Beliefs Limit Self-Confidence

There are many people who believe they can't get up in front of a group of people and give a dynamic talk; and they justify over and over again why they can't. This is another false belief which many people acquire through past conditioning.

False Beliefs Limit Memory Recall

A student can fail a subject he knows very well simply because of an examination. Students generally fear examinations. Their attitude is that examinations are difficult, strenuous, and sometimes "tricky." They feel they must cram or review extensively in order to have past learning available for the examination. As a result, fear of the examination itself can cause a good student to fail.

A student who knows he is going to have an examination on the lesson material will *subconsciously* not study the material properly until he is reviewing or cramming for an examination. He believes he will have to review the material before the examination anyhow, so he skims through his regular assignments, just hitting the high spots that will carry him safely through the class work. Each lesson that he does not study properly and thoroughly leaves him unprepared with no foundation to understand the succeeding lesson. Then just prior to an examination he is aware that he does not know the material and he tries to "cram" or review.

Students should study lesson material thoroughly and understand it as they go along. When they do this with the belief that they can recall everything as it is needed, they find they have no need to cram or review extensively for examinations because they know, understand, and recall all the material covered by the examination.

False Beliefs Limit Use of Talent

A child may grow up believing himself to be ignorant only because as a child he was called dumb or stupid. There are far too many cases where this is true. Parents often make this common mistake when a child does something foolish, and the child may go through life handicapped by a false belief which has been planted by an unwise remark.

If you catch yourself referring to a child as "stupid," a "dumb bunny," or similar comments when he does something foolish or awkward, continually inform the child that this is only an outlet, an expression of your impatience or anger, but that in reality he is good, he is smart, he is intelligent. Constantly tell him that you do love him and approve of him. If you develop this understanding with the child, then when you make rash comments in anger, the words have no effect other than expressing your anger or impatience with him. He knows that even though he is being reprimanded, you do not literally mean that he is dumb or stupid.

False Beliefs Limit Physical Ability

A person who has been injured in an accident and finds that he cannot walk right away may fear, or really believe, that he cannot ever walk again. This person may actually be unable to walk—not because of a physical impairment or disability, but only because of his fear or false belief. This false belief is fortified, of course, if the doctor tells him he may not or cannot walk.

On the other hand, there are many cases where a patient was told he would never walk again; but the patient believed so strongly that he would walk and was so determined to prove the doctors wrong that he did exactly that—he walked. This is the power of belief within you.

I know of one particular man who has a false hip. He was told he definitely would never be able to walk again, that it would be impossible for him to do so. And yet today he not only can walk, he can run, work, and do any and all things that anyone else can do.

Suggestions Are a Form of Self-Hypnosis

You receive suggestions from many, many sources. They come from parents, teachers, employers, friends, clergymen, advertising, news media, and many other areas—and even from yourself. It doesn't matter how or where you get the idea. The only thing that matters is whether you accept it as a fact and believe it to be true.

Any time you believe that an idea is true or that a statement made by someone else is true, it has the same power and effect upon you that a hypnotist's words have over his subject. And the only time a hypnotist, or anyone else, has any power over you is when you *believe* they have this power.

A Godsend to Mental Health

We would eliminate many problems in this world if parents would simply keep a family record or diary for a child and record everything pertinent to the child. The diary should include information relative to his training and teaching; what beliefs were taught him; what illnesses he had and what was suggested at the time as a diagnosis, treatment, and prognosis; and comments on any physical, mental, or emotional upset that the child might have such as falling from his crib or highchair, being frightened by the neighbor's dog, etc. If a child is disturbed or upset and you cannot determine the cause, you can still make a note that the child is disturbed on this particular day but the reason is unknown.

This record should be kept from the time of birth until the child is ten years of age. Usually from the age of ten on people can recall most things; but they frequently do not have good recall of things that happened before that age.

When the child is grown this record or diary should be given to him. If in later life he has a conflict or a mental or emotional problem of any kind, many times he can read through this diary and discover for himself what created the problem. And very often an understanding of the cause or source of a problem is all that is required to completely "cure" or remove it. If he seeks professional help, he can present the counsellor with this diary of his early childhood; and a competent counsellor could very often study the diary and know immediately where the problem originated. The diary would result in untold savings in time, money—and unhappiness—for this person. Family records would indeed be a godsend to mental health.

You Can Change Your Beliefs and Habits Without Effort

Your current beliefs, whether true or false, were actually created within you without effort. Your attitude and habits were formed without effort. Have you ever tried to break an unwanted habit and found you couldn't? You were defeated mainly because you *tried* to break it, you tried to use *will power, or effort;* and you failed.

The same holds true when learning a new habit. As I have explained, the conscious mind only makes the decision. It cannot force anything to be done immediately. You have to depend on your subconscious to do it for you.

You should understand and believe that you can change your habits, your self-image, your attitude—or, in other words, your beliefs—without conscious effort. This knowledge gives you more faith in yourself. Then you are well on your way to achieving your desires and becoming more successful.

The Four Basic Tools for Creating Success

The four basic tools you will use in order to be more successful are creative wording, creative imagination, acting-image, and repetition. There are others, of course, but these are the four major tools; these are the ones that get results for you.

In order to make these changes, to create successful habits and beliefs, it is necessary to learn more about these tools so you use them instead of them using you. You will soon become the master of these tools and never again a slave to them. In order for you to develop absolute faith in these tools you must uncover within yourself how you have been affected by them. Everyone is affected by them or uses them. When you examine your own fears and attitudes and begin to know yourself a little better by analyzing some of your habits and beliefs, take into consideration these tools we have talked about.

In the following chapters you will gain a thorough understanding of these four basic tools which you can use to change any facet. of your present self you wish to change. Remember: *creative wording, creative imagination, acting-image, and repetition.*

IMPORTANT POINTS TO RECALL

1. You must learn to recognize the present "you."
2. The "tools" which molded and forged the present "you" are the tools which will create the "new you" in the future.
3. Some of the basic causes of a neurosis are:
    a. Effect of Suggestion (or Power of Suggestion):
      (1) What you believe comes from sense impressions (sight, sound, touch, taste and smell).
      (2) You may not *consciously* recognize a suggestion or its effect.
      (3) The degree of suggestibility varies from individual to individual.
      (4) The effect of suggestion may work either for you or against you.
      (5) Suggestions are received from many outside sources, for example:

Parents	Advertising	Persons in Authority
Teachers	News Media	Public Figures
Doctors	Religion	Entertainment Personalities

      (6) Suggestions are accepted by the subconscious literally, word for word.
      (7) The power of suggestion is reinforced by repetition.
      (8) As adults we can use judgment to accept or reject suggestions; small children cannot.
      (9) The effect of suggestion is working constantly.
    b. Creative Wording
      (1) Creative wording is any phrase, statement, or series of words which explicitly expresses a presence, a condition, or a state of being as existing *here and now.*

(2) Creative wording creates an end result and many times it creates *an actual physical condition.*

(3) Through repetition, creative wording motivates the subconscious to react and materialize exactly what the words say. Results may be either good or bad for you.

(4) "I am going to," "I will," and "I'll try," imply doubt and are not explicitly "here and now"; therefore, they are not creative.

(5) Harmful creative wording is in common usage as a habit of speech.

(6) The key to the power of creative wording is repetition.

(7) Everyone is susceptible to the effect of creative wording.

c. Creative Imagination

(1) All imagination is not *creative* imagination. In *creative* imagination, YOU do the creating in your conscious mind.

(2) Fear is imagination using you.

(3) Creative imagination must be in vivid detail to motivate your subconscious to react and materialize anything.

(4) Creative imagination can be either beneficial or very destructive.

(5) The subconscious does not know the difference between a real experience and one created in vivid detail in your imagination.

d. Identification

(1) Children have a strong tendency to identify with someone possessing power or authority or someone loved.

(2) Identification causes imitation and dramatization, either consciously or unconsciously, of both physical and personality traits.

e. Past Experiences

(1) You are largely the product of your past experiences.

      (2) Past experiences are the root of many present fears.

   f. Conflicts

      (1) Both the conscious mind and the subconscious have the ability to think and they may agree or be in direct contradiction to each other.

      (2) This conflict can: defeat efforts to change unwanted habits; create guilt feelings; diminish self-confidence; color self-image; limit success.

4. Past conditioning and your reaction to it has created your present personality, attitude, self-image—or, in other words, your beliefs.

5. Many of your beliefs are inconsistent with the reality of now.

6. False beliefs impose many limitations.

7. Suggestions are a form of self-hypnosis.

8. Family records would be invaluable to mental health.

9. Beliefs, attitudes, and habits are acquired without effort—and you must learn to change them without effort.

10. The four basic tools for making these changes—and for creating future successes—are: creative wording, creative imagination, acting-image, and repetition.

CHAPTER THREE

Using Your Voice
to Achieve Success

In the preceding chapter about past conditioning you learned that people often use creative wording with no awareness of its power; and all too often they use it to create bad results, bringing harm to themselves. Now you shall learn how to use creative wording to create good results and achieve your goals.

There Is Only One Method That Works

We call this tool "creative" wording because there is a definite way to use words with repetition to get an end result; one method and one method only that really works. Let me refer you again to the definition of creative wording: creative wording is any phrase, statement, or series of words which explicitly expresses a presence, a condition, or a state of being as existing here and now. And I repeat again a point explained earlier, because it is very important that you understand this: creative wording does create an end result. Whether that end result is good or bad depends on how you use this tool.

A Better Understanding of Creative Wording

Let's gain a better understanding of creative wording by examining some examples of creative wording and non-creative wording. If you repeat the statement, "I am going to be successful," over and over again, you do not create anything at all. Even by using repetition with such a statement you still get no results because this type of statement is not creative wording and will create nothing.

Stop Thinking in Terms of "Positive" and "Negative"

Most people have come to interpret any statement which anticipates a good result as being "positive" and any statement which expresses an undesirable condition as being "negative." And in that light, they consider the statements, "I am going to be successful," or "I will be successful," as forceful, positive thinking. However, these statements are *not creative*. True, they reflect a pleasant attitude, but they will *create* nothing.

On the other hand, "I am tired," is almost universally considered to be a negative statement because it expresses an undesirable or "bad" physical condition. But in reality this is actually *creative* wording which conveys an explicit instruction to your subconscious; and if you repeat the words, "I am tired," often enough, your subconscious will react to this instruction and you will indeed be physically fatigued.

Beginning right now, discontinue thinking in terms of "positive" and "negative" and think only in terms of whether your words are *creative* or *non-creative* and whether the result from the creative wording will be a "good" result or a "bad" result.

"I Am Going to Be Successful"

Let's examine the statement, "I am going to be successful," and understand exactly what it says and why it is not creative, why it does not motivate your subconscious to take action to materialize success.

First of all, "I am *going to be* successful," implies you are *not successful at the present time*. If someone says, "I am going to be" a doctor, or fireman, or mechanic, or engineer, or anything else, he is saying that he is not one here and now but maybe some day he will be.

So by using this statement and repeating it over and over again you are affirming to your subconscious that you are not successful here and now, but maybe some day you are going to be. And "going to be" means some day, sometime—or just plain "maybe." Your subconscious cannot reason and does not know when that someday or sometime is supposed to be; and therefore it does not understand this statement as expressing your present true, sincere desire. It is not motivated to action and it does nothing to materialize anything for you. The only thing that is explicit or positive about "going to be" successful is that you are *not successful at the present time*.

"I Will Be Successful"

Again, if you say, "I will be successful," this is not explicit. It does not express that state of being or that condition as existing here and now. Your subconscious does not respond to this in any way because he has an out. "I will be," simply means that maybe you will be someday but it isn't necessary right now; so your subconscious doesn't have to go to work right now.

"I'll 'Try' to Be Successful"

Anytime you use the word "try" you are certainly implying doubt; and again you are giving your subconscious an out. Tell me, do you *try* to walk? Well, if you're in a wheel chair, perhaps you do. But the average person who is healthy and strong doesn't really *try* to walk, he just walks. Do you *try* to eat? Again, all things taken into consideration, the average person doesn't *try* to eat, he simply eats. Do you *try* to breathe, *try* to blink your eyes, or *try* to yawn? "Try" simply says you are not here and now doing something, that you have doubts about your ability to do it, but you might make an attempt to do it.

At best, such phrases as "try," "going to," "will be," etc., are nothing more than idle words with the potential of doing harm by repeatedly telling you that you are not successful *here and now.*

"I Am Successful"

But when you make the statement, "I am successful," then with repetition you certainly create success. This is creative wording: it is *explicit*; and it expresses a state of being as existing *here and now.* "I am successful." It says you are successful here and now and not at some nebulous time in the future. And because this statement is true creative wording, through repetition your subconscious accepts it as fact and is motivated to react to it and materialize success.

The spoken word definitely has a great power. But there is one thing absolutely certain: YOU must be the master and select the words you use. Then, and only then, will your words create *what you want.*

How to Give Your Words Power

No word in and of itself contains power. Power must be given to words by the one who speaks them. It is not absolutely necessary to have any thoughts behind creative wording in order for it to create the end result. The case histories cited in the chapter "How to Discover the Real You" are ample evidence to substantiate the fact that people often use words without conscious thought and still create the end result. However, the thought behind words certainly makes them more powerful.

Words possess meaning, and thinking of the meaning of the word does not strengthen or intensify the *meaning* of the word but it does add to the *power* that word has to create. For example, if you repeat "I am happy," over and over and over again without even thinking of the words, in time you certainly feel happy. However, if every time you say, "I am happy," you think of the meaning of the words you are saying and you *imagine* you are happy, you are joyous—your thoughts give more power to the words and you create happiness more rapidly.

A Literal Interpretation

Man is certainly the creator of words. Therefore, man has absolute control in selecting the words which he chooses to use. Man cannot invest a word or thought with any meaning outside of his own understanding of what the word means. Consequently every individual reacts to a word according to whatever he understands the word to mean—whatever it means to him.

If you say, "He gives me a headache," you intend to express disgust or disapproval; irritation; anger. But "headache" literally means "a pain in the head," and this is a meaning which has been made vividly clear to anyone who has ever experienced a severe headache. "Headache" does not mean "disgust, disapproval, irritation or anger," to me, and I seriously doubt that it does to anyone else. "Headache" means a "pain in the head," and when you say repeatedly, "He gives me a headache," your subconscious reacts exactly according to what the words mean to you—and you create a "pain in the head."

The average person does not understand what words really are or the power they convey. To him they are merely vehicles used to convey his thoughts to other people. You may ask, "How can I create a headache just by saying, 'He gives me a headache'? Those words don't say what I mean, so they are meaningless." It's true the words may not say what you really mean to say, but they do have a very literal meaning to your subconscious. They explicitly say that "he gives you a headache," and he does it right here and now—no "maybe" or "he'll try," or "he's going to," or "he will some day."

Think back for a moment. How many times have you or anyone else you may have overheard used an expression such as,

"He gives me a headache," "I can't stand it," "I can't swallow that," "He makes me sick," "He drives me crazy," and so forth, and spoken the words in an expressionless monotone, devoid of feeling or emphasis? This type of expression is almost always spoken with great emphasis, strong feeling, conviction, a great amount of expression and force—all of which strengthen the power of the words to create.

> "It makes a great difference in the force of a sentence whether a man be behind it or not."
>
> Ralph Waldo Emerson

Examples of Non-Creative Wording

When I speak of basic idle words, meaningless words, I am referring to expressions such as "going to," "will," and "try." These three basic idle words are used more commonly than any others. And these words create nothing. None of these statements is explicit; none of them clarifies where, when or how; none of them shows feeling, or conviction, or a true, sincere desire. And consequently, none of them creates anything. "I'll try," is perhaps the worst offender of all because it shows lack of faith in yourself, your abilities, your tremendous power as a conscious mind.

Although these statements may have a proper place in your everyday conversation, they are not true creative wording. They cannot create. And they cannot be used to retrain or master your subconscious.

Here and Now

You will soon make a list of the goals you yourself wish to achieve. Once you have set them down in writing you must decide which goal is most important to you at this time. This will probably be a long-range goal, which you will then break down into a series of short-range goals from which you will select your first step, or your first short-range goal.

To achieve this goal you will use creative wording, creative imagination, acting-image and repetition. The words you speak must convey the meaning that you *already have* the end result, that the condition or state of being which you desire exists here and now. When you make the statement, "I am going to be successful," you imply doubt and the state of being is not expressed as here and now. Take out these three words "going to be" and you have a creative statement: "I am successful." This is the type of statement which actually creates success.

You Cannot Lie to Your Subconscious

Now, this is sometimes confusing to people at first because they feel they are telling themselves a lie. But this is not so. Your subconscious cannot reason; and therefore, it does not define statements as being either true or false. Any creative statement you make is accepted by your subconscious as a statement of fact which expresses a condition, a presence, or a state of being. There is no question raised and no consideration given by the subconscious as to whether a statement is true or false—it is simply a fact. This has been proven time and time again through experiments.

For instance, if I place a man under hypnosis and say to him, "My desk is red, this desk is bright red," the man's subconscious cannot reason and it accepts my suggestion as fact. My desk is actually brown and the man consciously could see that the desk is brown; but until I release his subconscious from the suggestion that the desk is red, it accepts my statement and believes that the desk is red, and it reacts accordingly.

If this man is given a lie detector test while my suggestion that the desk is red still is dominant in his subconscious and if he is asked if the desk is red, he will answer, "Yes." He is not lying—and the lie detector will indicate that he is not lying—because his subconscious accepted my suggestion and believes that the desk is red.

If a subject named William is placed in deep hypnosis and given the suggestion: "Your name is John. It has been John all your life. You can recall playing with your playmates as a child and their calling you John or Johnny. Your birth certificate shows that your name is John," and if it is thus suggested in detail that his name is John, his subconscious reacts to this suggestion and accepts it as a fact. After the man awakens from hypnosis, if he is subjected to a lie detector test and asked if his name is William, he will say, "No," and the polygraph will indicate that he is telling the truth. If he is asked if his name is John, he will answer, "Yes," and the polygraph again will show that he is telling the truth, because his subconscious accepted the hypnotic suggestion as fact.

So when you express your goal as already being yours, as existing here and now, bear in mind that this is a method to achieve your goal, and a method only. You cannot *lie* to your subconscious.

If your goal is to be successful, don't take advantage of every lull in the conversation to announce, "I am successful," to your friends and co-workers. It is not necessary to repeat the suggestion for your goal in front of other people. By all means, though, do repeat it to yourself as often as possible to reinforce this suggestion to your subconscious and motivate it to take action to materialize your goal for you.

A Therapeutic Tool

As you recall, in the chapter "How to Discover the Real You," I showed you that creative wording is definitely a therapeutic tool; and I gave you examples of how people have created problems for themselves through misuse of this tool. We know that true creative wording definitely creates. You as an individual must be the master of your subconscious and get him to create what you want and to achieve your goals for you. In order to do this you must use these tools you are learning about.

Your Guide to Creating Success

There is a guide that must be followed by everyone who

desires a successful life. The first thing you must have is desire. Desire to be successful, desire to "get ahead," desire to get whatever you want out of life.

The second thing you must have is belief in these tools you are learning to use. You have to believe in these tools before you will use them. You have to believe that they definitely work before you will put them to work for you.

Third, you have to use these tools. You have to actually apply them and put them to work for you in order to achieve your goals.

Fourth, when you actually apply the tools, you feel the power in them; you feel that you are making accomplishments towards your goal. You feel yourself being motivated and accomplishing your goals.

Fifth, when you feel the motivation and the accomplishments, you develop absolute faith because you then have no doubts of any kind. You soon see the results of your accomplishments, and then you have:

Sixth, an end result.

1. Have desire.
2. Believe in the tools.
3. Use the tools.
4. Feel it.
5. Have absolute faith.
6. End result–SUCCESS.

This is a natural chain of events for everybody. You evidently have a desire to be successful, to improve, or you wouldn't have purchased this book. And now you are learning to understand these tools and to believe in them so you will be able to use them. It will be proven to you, to your own individual self, that these tools do work, that they are indeed very effective. You are now learning how to use creative wording correctly in order to get results.

Only YOU Instruct Your Subconscious

Your subconscious acts only on the instructions *you* really give it. Regardless of where these instructions come from, in a sense *you accept them* and then you convey them to your subconscious. Your subconscious cannot reason as your conscious mind does. It does not know and cannot decide what is good for you or what is bad for you.

For instance, take a man who constantly repeats, "I am a failure," or "The world is against me," and you will find a man who *is* a failure or whom the world *does* seem to "be against." He is expressing these words with feeling and impressing them upon his subconscious. His subconscious accepts these words as an instruction expressing his sincere desire; and it will make sure in the future that he continues to fail or the world continues to "be against him." He is actually using creative wording to achieve a very bad result.

Blue Monday

Many people think Monday is a "bad" day. They have just had a weekend of leisure time or time spent doing things they enjoy and now they have to go back to work. So these people develop a habit of saying and thinking that Monday is always a bad day. They dread Mondays. They hate Mondays. And with this attitude they actually create a bad day every Monday—not because their job duties are more taxing or different from any other day, but simply because they continually say and think, as a habit, that Monday is a rotten day.

These people ruin a whole day just because they have this attitude and they get to the point where they actually do hate Monday. But Tuesday doesn't seem to really bother them even though it requires the same amount of work and effort and follows the same routine as Monday.

Begin thinking and talking about Monday as though it's a very important and pleasant day of the week. Carry the thought that you enjoy Monday, that Monday is very important to you because it is another whole day which you can use to progress towards your goals. If you adopt this new thinking and new manner of speaking about Monday as a habit, you can change your "Blue Monday" into another very pleasant and profitable day.

A "Hard Luck" Failure

People always set out to prove they are right, that what they believe is true—even though the results may be harmful to them—because their subconscious acts upon these beliefs to make them a reality. The man who says, "I am a failure," is using this powerful tool to defeat himself. Regardless of how much ability the man has, if he continues to use creative wording in such a harmful, destructive way, he will always be a "hard luck" failure. He must change his words and thoughts to get himself out of a rut. He must replace them with words and thoughts which get him going on the road to success and which create the things he wants rather than things which are harmful and limiting.

It's Simple

It is surprising and disturbing to realize how very few people really control themselves. Creative wording is so simple a child can understand it—and often does.

You now have an advantage most others do not. You are aware of these powers you have. And remember, you are not learning how to get these powers—you already have them. You are only learning to recognize that you do have them, to realize the power these tools give you, and learning how to use them to create success.

The Power of Words Affirmed

Let's continue to build more proof of the existence and power of creative wording. The New Testament offers additional evidence that words are powerful. "For by thy words thou shalt be justified, and by thy words thou shalt be condemned." (Matthew 12:37) This is a biblical statement of what we now know about creative wording. Our subconscious reacts to our words and justifies our beliefs by creating what we say; and when we use words unwisely, we are condemned to an existence created with our very own words.

Remember, words alone do create when they are used as true creative wording. As we discussed before, the thought behind the words certainly makes the words more powerful and brings faster response from your subconscious. But words alone can and do create an end result—according to the exact meaning of the words we speak—when they are used as creative wording.

The Bible also tells us: "There is nothing from without a man that entering into him can defoul him, but the things which come out of him, those are they that defoul the man." (Mark 7:15) This is another reference to the words which come out of our mouths.

And still another scripture says: "For verily I say unto you that whosoever shall say unto this mountain be thou removed and be thou cast into the sea, and shall not doubt in his heart, but shall believe that those things which he sayeth shall come to pass, he shall have whatsoever he sayeth." (Mark 11:23) Words again, and a testimony to their incredible power.

"I Am Happy"

Do you have any doubts that your words can move mountains? Is there any question that creative wording is really very effective? Can you question these words?

If you do, here's a little experiment which you may try yourself. Repeat the following over and over and over again consistently: "I am happy, happy, happy, happy." Continue repeating this at every possible opportunity until you feel the effects, until you feel happy. Do it until a time comes when you feel a little depressed and just by saying, "Happy, happy, happy," you come completely out of your depression.

This is just a very tiny example of the tremendous power

words have to create. And remember, when you say, "I am happy, happy, happy, happy," imagine yourself as being extremely happy. Imagine pleasant circumstances; imagine that everything in your life is perfect, just the way you want it. You will be amazed at the results.

Creative Wording for Many Areas of Life

Let me give you some examples of proper creative wording which you may use in many areas of your life: I am perfect health. I am happy. I am successful. I make friends easily. I speak fluently. I enjoy people. People enjoy me. I like people. I am relaxed. I create my own future. I learn every day. I progress faster every day. I recall everything as I need it.

All these statements, and many, many more, are definitely creative wording; and they certainly create an end result if they are repeated over and over again enough times. Proper creative wording as shown in these examples is what you must use, together with creative imagination, acting-image, and repetition, to achieve your future successes. No matter what your goal may be, no matter what you want in life, you can have it by using these tools. This is how powerful you really are.

Use the Basic Tools in Conjunction with Each Other

Use these basic tools in conjunction with each other. When you say, "I am happy," think that you are happy. Be exuberant when you say it: "I am happy; oh my, but I am happy. I feel good. I feel great." Imagine that you feel good; imagine that you feel great; imagine that you feel free and clear all over, and that you've never felt better in your life. Act as if you are happy. Act exuberant and enthused. Act as though you feel marvelous.

Repeat these words, thoughts and actions over and over, and over and over again, many times each and every day; and the end results are yours.

A Reminder

Always remember that to accomplish your goals you have to express your goals in your words, imagination, and actions as being "here and now," never in the future. Then have no doubts and your goals, the things you desire, are yours—and it's really that simple.

Never use such words as, "I am going to," "I will," or "I'll try," because these words always postpone anything to an indefinite time. They never pin it down for action.

Do Not Set Time Limits

Do not impose time limits on reaching your goals. If you say, "I am going to be successful tomorrow," and tomorrow you are not successful, then you have defeated yourself. You have to develop faith that is not based on a specific time limit. There are a million and one things which could happen that might delay a goal for a few days longer or even a few weeks, but still you would be assured of achieving your goal if you did not set a time limit and defeat yourself.

So do not set any time limits on your goals. Do not say, "I am going to have a million dollars in one year," because a year later if you do not have your million dollars you feel, "Well, these things don't work"; and you give up. Maybe you would have gotten the million dollars in 15 months. But if you didn't get it by the time you set as your time limit—and 99 times out of 100 you won't—then you would give up and quit trying, and the million dollars would never be yours. Not only that, perhaps you could have had the million dollars in nine months; but you wouldn't get it in nine months because you specified one year. Thus, you have defeated yourself again.

My reason for saying that 99 times out of 100 you will not have reached your goal by the end of your time limit is very simple. Your subconscious cannot reason. Therefore, he cannot apply reasoning and say, "If he wants this in six months, I'd better start working on it right away." Also, if you say, "I will be successful in six months," and a week later you again say, "I will be successful in six months," as far as your subconscious is concerned you have changed your deadline. "In six months" does not mean August 25th to him, or any other particular day. It means six months from the day he receives the instruction.

Then again, if you set a specific date—such as, "I will be successful by December 20th"—you are actually giving your subconscious an instruction that you are not successful now and won't be before December 20th. Your subconscious takes your words literally; and since you have instructed him that you won't be successful before December 20th, he takes no action to fulfill your desire until then. So remember: do not set any time limits for achieving your goals. Time limits will only defeat you.

Don't Look for Immediate Results

Never look for immediate results. Remember, you want to build successful habits and faith that you can have anything you want. At first you may have the feeling that you are merely repeating words; but very soon you begin to feel the power of the words. And when you can actually feel the power of your own words, you become motivated, you feel enthusiasm, and your thoughts are constructive thoughts which further contribute to your future success.

You have to use creative wording many times each and every day in the form of a habit for it to be effective.

An Aid

A little aid in achieving results during the day would be to type up your creatively worded suggestion on a three-by-five card and carry it with you. When you do this, you are reminded of your goal; and you can read your suggestion out loud many times a day.

No Struggle or Effort Required

Practice and use these tools and results are yours. Using them becomes a habit, and in a few months you use them automatically with no effort at all. You do not have to force your subconscious to work for you. He is always there, ready, willing, and able to materialize whatever you desire. In fact, he works miracles when you give him something to work on. He really doesn't like to work for other people, so put him to work for you—nobody else. Practice using these tools you are learning about until you create a new and wonderful habit; and then you accomplish those things which create a successful future.

Accomplishing your own desires requires no struggle or effort. Just carry the correct thought; use the correct words, out loud, repeated over and over many times; and soon this becomes automatic, a habit, without effort of any kind. All obstacles are removed and you are well on your way to getting what you want in life.

Your First Duty

One of your first duties is to prove to yourself the value, the effectiveness, and the power of these tools. If you search into your own habits and your own thoughts and words, you will discover that you, too, are using creative wording as a habit and that you, too, have created the end result.

"He Gets Under My Skin"

I gave you examples earlier of people who say he or she "gets under my skin," as a habit of speech, and they actually create a skin disease, sometimes even in the form of psoriasis. This condition they have created certainly can be cured by those people when they stop using harmful creative wording and create another habit of speech using a statement that benefits them. Then their skin clears up and they feel fine.

This is no fantasy. Under therapeutic conditions many patients have been referred for psychotherapy because they had skin diseases which would not respond to medical treatment.

I had a young fellow in one of my classes one time who had hands which looked gravelly, or like they were covered with sandpaper. This man used the words, "He gets under my skin," continually. I would estimate that he repeated that statement twenty times a day. From my classes this man learned to understand the power of words and how, through his own words, he had created this unpleasant condition. He stopped using this very harmful expression and replaced that habit of speech with words which would benefit him. His hands were actually clear in less than two months' time.

Don't "Damn" Yourself

There are many people who have a habit of saying, "I'll be damned," and this habit of speech will create a "damned" existence for these people. Dig out your own statements and find out what you are saying to yourself.

Creative Wording for All Areas of Life

When you find that you are using creative wording which is harmful to you, replace it with a habit of speech that creates "good" in your life. Here are just a few examples of creative wording you may use to create good results in each of the basic areas of life—spiritual, mental, physical, social, financial, and family life:

I serve others.	I am prosperous.
I am needed.	I am successful.
I am motivated.	I am wealthy.
I am loved.	I am strong.
I am peaceful.	I feel good.
I am energetic.	I am perfect health.
I am happy.	I have perfect vision.
I am confident.	I am pleased with myself.

I am determined.   I am relaxed.

I am patient.   **I am free and clear.

**(This is a statement devised to remove soreness and pain. Instead of saying, "I have no soreness or pain," you use the words "free and clear." In this way you do not acknowledge or recognize the existence of soreness or pain.)

Remove Bad Conditioning and False Beliefs

Once you understand how the present "you" has been created by your past conditioning, and once you know the part these tools have played in this past conditioning, then you can use these very same tools to remove bad conditioning and false beliefs.

I have had reports from many people who were mentally disturbed who actually were cured completely, with no recurrence, just by reading my earlier book, *Your Inner Magic,* and applying the principles it contains. It seems that when people gain knowledge and an understanding of themselves and their problems, their subconscious oftentimes reacts to this new knowledge and understanding by removing the problem.

That is really what psychoanalysis consists of. When you go to a psychoanalyst for help, he looks for something which happened in your life—most often in your childhood or formative years—and he looks for harmful creative wording.

Most of the basic causes of a neurosis which we talked about earlier are actually used as tools to create the future you want. We know these tools are effective; we know they get results. These tools can create "bad" results; and therefore we know they can also create "good" results. We know we can use them to create what we want, to get whatever we want in life.

Remove Your Attitude of Negativism

We have created an attitude of negativism in our thoughts;

and all too often we express this negative attitude in our own words. There is no need to go into a lengthy discussion or analysis of the basis for this attitude, but it is extremely important that you recognize its existence and then change this pattern of thought and speech in your own life.

We express this negative attitude in every area of our lives, from the most important to the least significant. We use it almost as though we believe we can create some reversed effect and by expressing what we don't want we can ward off or deceive some evil spirit and receive what we want instead of what we say or think. Sometimes we use negative statements in the misguided belief that it shows humility or self-effacement. Sometimes we use them because they express our own false self-image.

How many people, upon contracting some minor illness, allow their imagination to run rampant, completely out of control, and conjure up horrendous thoughts of dreaded diseases, incapacitating illness, insurmountable medical expenses? And they express these fears in words. This is the very time when they should use the tremendous power of words and imagination to affirm that they are perfect health.

How many women carrying a child express fears, either secretly in their thoughts or sometimes openly in their words, that the baby may have a physical or mental infirmity, the baby may be stillborn, or there may be a serious complication in delivery? Perhaps these women create nothing more than needless fears and anxieties by their thoughts and words, but these alone are detrimental to the physical and mental health of both the mother and the unborn child. And this is a time when more than any other time in her life a woman should use the power of words and imagination to affirm, "I am perfect health. My baby is perfect health and bodily perfection."

The last time you took a driving test, how many times did you think or say, "I always have trouble with the written part." "I know all the rules and everything but I get confused and I can't remember them when I take that darned test." "I'll probably get so rattled I'll even flunk the driving part." And if you're especially imaginative you may even envision the possibility of doing something particularly inept such as having an accident during the driving examination. Whenever you have an examination or test of any type, use this tool, this tremendous power of creative wording, to affirm, "I am qualified. I am capable. I am confident. I recall everything as I need it."

True, you do not have a child, become ill, or take a test every day. But these are important occasions in your life. Why should you allow this attitude of negativism to create doubts and fears and rob you of your self-confidence and judgment? Instead, take advantage of these opportunities to use your God-given powers to help you create "good" successes instead of allowing your imagination and words to control you and create "bad" successes.

Have you ever gone on a picnic or other kind of outing when someone in your party didn't say, "It's going to rain," or "It will probably be too cold"? How many seasons have changed without a million people grousing, "It will probably be another hot, miserable summer," or "It's going to be a cold, miserable winter"? We carry this attitude of negativism into even the smallest, most insignificant areas of our life. We keep a large supply of well-worn statements such as "Nothing really good ever happens to me," "I couldn't possibly be that lucky," "That would be just too good to be true," "Not with my luck, it won't," "Nothing ever turns out the way you plan," "Something always happens at the last minute to spoil things," and on, and on, and on.

You eat a favorite food and say, "It always gives me indigestion." You play cards and say, "My cards are just never there." You go shopping and say, "I can never find what I want." You cheer yourself hoarse for your team to make that touchdown; and all the time you're cheering as the player runs down the field towards the goal post, you keep saying, "He'll never make it. He'll never be able to do it." You have a hope or a dream or a plan of some sort, but your thoughts and your words are that "It won't work out. Nothing will ever come of it."

Examine your own thoughts and words. I believe you will be surprised and appalled to realize just how often you express this negative attitude each and every day of your life, and to what extremes you carry this attitude in applying it even to the most trivial incidents. Some of these statements are not true creative wording; but by using them you create a habit of negativism and you continually use your thoughts and your words to express defeat and failure.

You're afraid to hope for success so you express failure. And you turn these opportunities for using thoughts and words to create good for yourself into nothingness, idle words and thoughts; or you reinforce this attitude of defeat and failure, you undermine your self-confidence, and you deny for that moment the power of these tools which you have at your command and with which you can create anything you desire.

You Create Your Own Existence

This is the power you have within you as an individual. You can create anything you want to create. You do have these powers and you had better make good use of them.

Too many people unknowingly allow their minds to be used against them. As I have said before, your subconscious acts only on instructions which you allow it to act upon. Even when you were only six months of age you accepted certain things as fact. Today you may not even recall them, but nevertheless you did accept them and your subconscious may still be reacting to them. When you accepted these things as facts, they were either suggestions, creative wording, or creative imagination which you yourself imagined. Therefore, you have created your own existence—you have created your own habits and your own beliefs.

Recognize Your Power—Then Use It

Most people are not aware of the existence of these tools, even though they use them every day of their lives. The whole purpose of this book is to teach you to recognize the power you have and which you use every day—sometimes for your betterment, but all too frequently to your own detriment. When you recognize these tools and this power, then you can master your future instead of allowing your future to "just happen" because of your unawareness. You do have this power. Now it's time to put it to use for a great and wonderful future.

IMPORTANT POINTS TO RECALL

1. Creative wording can achieve either good results or bad results, depending on how you use it.
2. There is only one method of using words with repetition to get an end result.
3. Creative wording must express your goal as existing here and now, as already being yours. "Going to," "will," and "try" are not creative wording.
4. The thought behind the words makes them more powerful; but words alone will create an end result.
5. Every individual reacts to a word according to his own exact understanding of the literal meaning.
6. Repetition is very important to the effectiveness of creative wording. Creative wording must be used in the form of a habit to be effective.
7. You cannot lie to your subconscious.
8. Your subconscious acts only on the instructions *you* give it.
9. Never impose time limits for achieving goals.
10. Creative wording has played a major role in creating your past and will play a far more important role in creating your future.
11. You must be the master and use creative wording properly to reach your goals.

CHAPTER FOUR

Creating Success Patterns

"The human race is governed by its imagination."

Napoleon Bonaparte

One of the basic tools you have at your command is creative imagination. Most people never know how powerful and amazing this tool really is or what a great role creative imagination plays in our lives.

Unfortunately, however, most of the time people do not command or control this tool at all, but rather they let it create whatever it wants. And without control and guidance our imagination frequently creates unnecessary and unrealistic fears and anxieties which not only make us unhappy and discontented, but which prevent us from achieving our goals and being free, successful individuals.

YOU Do the Creating

We call this tool "creative" imagination because it is something you must create yourself in your conscious mind. As a conscious mind you use your creative imagination to form a mental picture of your goal; and then through repetition of this mental picture you get your subconscious to materialize it.

Real Experience vs. Imagined Experience

You create these mental pictures of what you desire. And when you as a conscious mind create a mental picture, repeating it over and over again many times, your subconscious reacts to it—mainly because the subconscious cannot reason and cannot tell the difference between what is real and what is imagined in vivid detail and it reacts to either as a real experience.

The great significance of this fact and the potential power available to us by using this for our own advantage and growth may not be apparent to you immediately. But as you read on you see how very vital this tool can be in removing undesirable habits and creating the future you desire. Remember: Your subconscious cannot tell the difference between a real experience and one you imagine in your conscious mind in vivid detail; and *it reacts to both as a real experience.*

Repetition

In using creative imagination we again employ the tool repetition. It is important to understand that you must use repetition in conjunction with creative imagination, because it is this combination of tools you use to recondition your subconscious.

Most Powerful Tool to Create Success

"Imagination is more important than knowledge."

Albert Einstein

As stated earlier, creative imagination is a basic tool, and it is one of the greatest tools we have at our command. Imagination is not only the most powerful tool to get what we want in life, but it is also the most powerful tool to *prevent* us from getting what we want. It is one of those tools which can hold us back and cause many, many problems. This, of course, depends on who does the controlling, you or your subconscious.

The main reason that imagination is the most powerful tool we have at our command is because our mind always operates in picture form. Everything we think and say is in picture form in our mind before it's made into a reality.

From Fantasy to Reality

As a child I used to go to the movies almost every Saturday afternoon and watch the short serials. I watched Flash Gordon, Buck Rogers, Dick Tracy, and all those "way out" movies.

I was fascinated by all the amazing things those movies showed. Of course, no one in those days ever dreamed that the fantastic figments of the writers' imaginations shown in those movies would ever become reality. And yet today almost everything I saw then which was considered unbelievable and impossible, nothing more than a "way out" idea, has come to pass. Some of these things are now considered to be common conveniences of everyday life, or unremarkable and logical products of modern science and technology. Even during World War II there were many who thought airplanes without propellors would never get off the ground; and look what we have today.

"Around the World in 80 Days"

Jules Verne (1828-1905) became known throughout the world for his unlimited creative imagination which he used in his writing. It was Jules Verne who, way back in the 1800's, wrote all about automobiles, airplanes, submarines, and even atomic power. Although he hardly ever left the quiet of his home, during his lifetime he wrote tales of voyages and adventures in which the possibilities of modern science were treated in an unbelievably exaggerated manner which staggered the imagination and stretched the credulity of all who read his books.

A Man of Vision

But he wrote with truly marvelous vision. It is noteworthy that some of the things which the imagination of Verne created and which strained the credulity of his readers—the airplane, the submarine, and the automobile—are now accomplished facts; and science has progressed even far beyond that. When people scoffed at his ideas, Jules Verne retorted: "Whatever one man is capable of conceiving, other men will be able to achieve." And now our new "Nautilus" is a prototype of Verne's imaginary submarine.

Well-known among Verne's stories are "Twenty Thousand Leagues Under the Sea," "Around the World in 80 Days," "The Mysterious Island," "From the Earth to the Moon," and "Five Weeks in a Balloon." All of these stories have been made into great and popular movies.

Creative Imagination Is in Vivid Detail

What an imagination he had! And what vivid, minute detail he had in his imagination. Now, this is important: what *detail* he had in his imagination. Today people marvel at his thoughts: "My, what an imagination he had." Some people even remark that perhaps he had visions of the future or some mysterious insight. Few people realize that all he really did was use his creative imagination in vivid detail.

Two Heads ARE Better Than One

Let me interject an explanation here as to why many of Jules Verne's dreams have come true. He was a writer and thousands of people read his books. Many thousands more saw the movies made from the books. So in addition to his own imagination, there were actually millions of other people who envisioned or created these same things in their own imaginations, both during and after reading his books or seeing the movies made from them.

Imagination certainly creates much faster with more people using it for the same purpose. We know for a fact that two people imagining the same thing cause it to be a fact faster than one person; 50 create faster than 2; 1,000 much faster than 50; and a million much faster than a thousand. This is no doubt the single biggest reason for the great speed with which the creations of Jules Verne's imagination came to be accomplished facts.

I know of no better illustration to demonstrate the power of imagination than to cite Jules Verne as an example. If you examine all of the things he created in his imagination and compare them with what we have today, you can see for yourself how powerful imagination can be.

Invent—"To Create or Devise in the Imagination" (Webster)

All of the world's great scholars and inventors used their imagination; and the very things they wrote about and created in their minds have generally all come to pass. When we speak of inventors, there is a never-ending chain of men and women who use their imagination to create a vast array of products and advancements for the comfort and benefit of mankind.

I could sit down and imagine many things, knowing that all of them could come to be a reality if I really wanted them to. Basically I wouldn't do this because I have personal goals and I use my imagination to achieve my own goals. But I do imagine in vivid detail, one goal at a time until I achieve it; and then I go on to another goal.

YOU Can Create with Your Imagination

Can *you* do this with your imagination? Of course, you can. It doesn't matter who you are, you can use your imagination to create anything you want. Now, take just a minute and stop to realize that any true, sincere desire you have can become a reality, no matter what it is. Let me repeat that: Any of the things you create in your imagination in vivid detail with a strong, sincere desire, can be yours in reality.

Creative Imagination Can Work Against You

The power of imagination can definitely work against people as well as for them. There are many people who imagine an accident of some type; and, of course, when the accident occurs they say, "See, I told you it would happen. I knew it would happen."

There are people who imagine getting turned down for a job or a raise, and they are absolutely sure this is exactly what will happen. They are right, of course, because they not only imagine it, they feel it; and they actually set out to prove they are right, because they imagine it in vivid detail. People imagine many things which can do them harm, such as fear of darkness, fear of failure, jealousy, and so on. In reality they create the very same thing they imagine.

"Things Always Happen in Threes"

Many people consistently make their plans based on what they "think" will happen. And they imagine both good and bad circumstances—but mostly bad. Some people persist in believing that things "always happen in threes," such as airline crashes. And they frequently do happen in threes—but not because of some mystical power held by the number three.

Whenever a prominent public figure or someone from the entertainment world dies, how many thousands of people think and say, "Oh my, I wonder who will be next; these things always happen in threes, you know." When the newspaper headlines carry the news of the horrible tragedy of an airliner crashing, thousands upon thousands of people say, "Isn't it terrible? And there's bound to be another one soon because these things always happen in threes."

So we have many thousands of people all using the power of their creative imagination, and the power of creative wording, imagining in vivid detail, and saying with conviction and feeling, that there will be another accident, another death, another crash, because "things always happen in threes"—and these thousands of powerful minds can, and frequently do, create what is being imagined in vivid detail, even though it may be another tragedy.

Fear Creates That Which Is Feared

Fear is the strongest form of imagination which uses people. Fear of war actually creates war. Just stop and think how many people in this world today actually think of war and fear war.

Fear of bad health actually creates bad health. Again, consider for a moment how many people get a slight cold and begin immediately to think of themselves as being more ill than they really are. How many people fear, almost to the point of obsession, that they will get cancer, develop heart trouble, and on and on.

You Must Be the Master

It is important for you to understand that these people are letting imagination use them. They are not controlling it, they are not using it the way they should. Their conscious minds should be the master. They should use imagination to get the things they want out of life instead of creating fears and anxieties. Everytime you let your imagination use you, you are letting your prior conditioning tell you what to do. You are letting your subconscious, which cannot reason, guide your life. You are letting him run the show in any way he desires; and it's high time you made a change and began to show him who's boss.

Who Is the Boss?

Who is the boss, you or your subconscious? Are you letting

this animal part of you control your life? You can and must always control your imagination. It functions the way it does now because of force of habit. You have to change these habits. Never again let imagination run you. Never let your subconscious control your thoughts. You are the master: act the part.

Mental Pictures

When you begin to set your goals down in writing, you will be working on that first step towards what you want in life. You will then plan what kind of mental pictures you must continually carry—at least until you achieve that very first step. These mental pictures in your conscious mind will be the pictures of the end result you want and they help create that end result.

Here and Now

This is why everything must be imagined as though it were already an accomplished fact. Just as with creative wording, creative imagination must be used to imagine the condition or state of being which you desire as already existing *here and now.* This is the only way that you can possibly create that end result—imagine it in vivid detail as already existing. This is the power you have through creative imagination and this is how you use this power to achieve what you want.

Fear Is in Vivid Detail

By understanding fear and knowing that fear is something you create in vivid detail in your imagination, you can understand why and how imagination works so well. There are many people who can't create anything in their imagination except trouble, because they really don't know how to use it correctly. They don't know how to create what they want.

Create No Fear for Tomorrow

Why should you worry about things days and weeks before they even happen? Even in the Bible we are told to, "Take no thought for the morrow," and this is excellent advise. Do not take thought for the morrow; and especially, create no *fear* for the morrow.

Expressing your goals in your words and in your imagination as already being yours, as existing *here and now*, helps you to avoid creating fears or anxieties for their fulfillment or "for the morrow." When you say and think, "I have it now. It's already mine," then you eliminate anxieties about when and how you will get it and you avoid unnecessary fears that you may not accomplish it. These fears and anxieties are completely unnecessary, because when you use the four major tools properly, you can create any success you desire.

Fear of Rejection

Let's take a common occurrence and see how you can put your creative imagination to work either for you or against you—and what the results will be in each instance.

Suppose you want a pay raise from your employer. You work hard, you are capable in your work and you do it well, you have been in your present position for a sufficient length of time, and you feel you are entitled to more money. You begin to mentally practice just how to approach your boss with your request for a raise.

Perhaps in your "mental practice" you do not control your imagination but let it wander in any direction. Through your past conditioning you have developed a habit of allowing your imagination to create fears; and because of your lack of control, it now begins to create little doubts, little fears. You imagine that "with your luck" you catch the boss when he is in a bad mood and he is not receptive to your request. You imagine that the company has had a slow year financially and the boss says they just can't afford to give you a raise right now. You imagine that the boss may not, after all, have any idea how hard you work or how capable you are, and he doesn't even think you're entitled to a raise.

And you continue to imagine countless other reasons why your request for a raise will be denied. You create such a fear of your request being refused that you may even decide it's pointless to ask for a raise which in reality you are truly entitled to. If you follow through with your plan and present your request, you may do so almost apologetically because of your fear of refusal. Or again, because you have created a fear of refusal and you are already angry over a rejection that has not yet taken place, you may present your request in a belligerent, demanding manner.

In either case, every time you have mentally practiced your approach to the situation, every time you have imagined this particular experience, you have imagined failure. You have created fear—and you very likely have also created failure. You have not controlled your imagination but have allowed it to control you and limit you with very unhappy results.

Suppose, however, that you do control your imagination. When you mentally practice just how you will approach the boss and what his response will be, you imagine he is in a relaxed, congenial frame of mind. You know that you work hard and well and you know that the boss is aware of this fact and appreciative of your efforts. Every time you mentally practice or imagine this experience of asking for a raise, you imagine yourself as presenting your request in a concise, self-assured, positive manner; and you imagine the boss expressing his approval of your work, recognizing the merits of your request and granting the raise. You imagine success rather than failure—and you create success instead of failure.

Cancel Out Bad Thoughts

The last time you took a vacation and you drove your car, how many times did you or some member of your family imagine some accident, a flat tire, being stranded along the road in the dark, missing a turn and being on the wrong road, running out of gas, or having mechanical problems?

When undesirable thoughts occur to you or are expressed by those around you, immediately create a new thought to cancel out the bad one. You should imagine that the trip is very enjoyable with no problems of any kind, and that you arrive at your destination safe and sound after a very pleasurable journey. Imagination is powerful, but you must do the creating and create what you want instead of creating fears and harmful results.

Don't Make a Habit of Fear

We all use our imaginations each and every day to create fears—fears which at the very best are deplorable wastes of time, energy, and this marvelous tool, creative imagination.

It's true that many of these fears are small. The bride fears tripping on the way down the aisle. The groom is afraid he will drop the ring. The hostess fears her garden party will be washed away by a sudden downpour. The student fears tests. The homemaker fears the cake will fall. The husband fears the old car won't hang together until the last payment is made. The young girl fears she will be a wallflower. The young boy fears he won't make the team.

We develop a habit of fear and the fears grow. A very small child has no fear. He is not born with fear; he learns fear. And fear, like anything else, develops or grows with practice. Our fears grow in the scope and in the detail and vividness with which we are capable of imagining them—and we develop our ability to create what we fear.

Examine Your Own Fears

Examine yourself and be aware of the fears you create, both large and small, in your imagination and the expression you give to these fears with your words. How many unfounded fears have you imagined in just the past week? How many times have you thought or said, "I'm afraid I'm catching a cold." "I'm afraid another cup of coffee will keep me awake." "I'm afraid it will rain." "I'm afraid he is really more sick than he lets on." "I'm afraid the furnace won't last through the winter." "I'm afraid we can't afford a vacation next summer." "I'm afraid he won't like it." "I'm afraid she won't understand." "I'm afraid I will get cancer if I don't stop smoking." "I'm afraid Johnny will have an accident if we let him take the car." "I'm afraid the doctor will want to put me in the hospital and we just can't afford it right now."

We fill our lives with fears of all sizes and shapes, fears that range from the ridiculous to the horrible. I would feel that every atom of thought and energy which has gone into the writing of this book has been most generously rewarded if I could accomplish nothing more than to impel you to become aware of the fears which you allow your imagination to create.

You must understand that these fears create. Creative imagination does create an end result. And when you allow your imagination to wander without direction and control, it continues to respond to the habit of fear and you create what you fear. You must begin now to control your imagination and to use it to create success instead of fear and failure. Use your creative imagination to create the future you desire.

Practice Makes Perfect—In Your Imagination

For several years psychologists have done series of many different types of tests to show the powers of creative imagination. One of the most popular of these tests consists of taking several teams and having them practice in different ways.

Let's take the example of three basketball teams: teams A, B, and C. Team A was instructed to practice daily on the basketball court before the basketball season began. And they did exactly that: each day they practiced faithfully on the court.

Team B was instructed to practice only in their imagination and to imagine a perfect game each and every time. They were to do this imaginary practice for the same length of time that team A would practice on the court.

Team C was instructed not to practice either way: neither on the court nor in their imagination.

When the basketball season arrived and the real games were played, teams A and B were almost identical in ability. But team B was actually superior and was able to play and win more games because they had practiced *perfection* in their imagination.

These tests are additional proof that the subconscious cannot reason. It could not tell the difference between a real practice session and one practiced in vivid detail in their imagination.

How to Improve Your Golf Score

Many books have been written about the game of golf which advise you to practice golf in your imagination. Many times people who were in the hospital or who had a broken arm or leg and could not play golf would practice a game of golf every day, or whenever they could, in their imagination. If they had been having difficulty with a certain swing, they would practice performing the swing perfectly in vivid detail in their imagination.

When they recovered from their illness and were able to play golf again, they would go out on the course and discover they had actually improved their game, simply through practicing in their imagination. Even people who were already excellent golfers found they had improved their score by practicing in their imagination. Again, additional proof as to the power of creative imagination when used in vivid detail.

Only YOU Limit Your Imagination

When creative imagination is used in health matters, it works wonders. When it is used in business matters, it words wonders. When it is used to condition and control the subconscious properly, it has no limits of any kind. Who can place a limitation on our imagination?

How to Exercise Through Imagination

Let me elaborate on the power of creative imagination and prove to you that you do create an end result when you imagine in vivid detail. Learn to exercise in your imagination by creating a mental picture in absolute, vivid detail. Bicycling is an excellent form of exercise for your overall physical self. So lie down and relax; and in your imagination take a ride on a bicycle.

First, imagine the bicycle you are going to ride; the type, size, and color; what kind of seat and handlebars it has; whether it has hand brakes, or maybe a carrying basket. Perhaps you can even visualize a brand name.

Is the bicycle in the garage or carport? See yourself take hold of the handlebars, pull up the kick stand and wheel the bicycle out to the driveway. Imagine yourself getting on the bike and beginning to pedal down the driveway onto the sidewalk or over the curb to the street. Take your time and imagine all the details. In your imagination actually see yourself pedalling, see the wheels turning. Feel the handlebars in your hands and feel your legs moving.

Choose the route you are going to travel on your ride and imagine the houses, the yards and the people, and maybe even a dog barking as you ride past. Imagine the kind of day it is and feel the warmth of the sun or maybe a cool, refreshing breeze blowing in your face.

A Word of Caution

Continue your ride for maybe 15 or 20 minutes. I give you a word of caution, though: do not overdo it. If you do, your legs will be sore from too much exercise. This may be difficult for you to believe at first; but if you ride too long, you will soon find out just how sore your legs will be.

Your Subconscious Believes

Today it is a well-known fact in medicine that when you exercise in vivid detail in your imagination, your body chemistry makes changes and adjustments almost identical to those caused by actual physical exercise. Since your subconscious cannot reason and cannot distinguish a real experience from one imagined in vivid detail, your subconscious believes you have exercised and it reacts to this belief. And since your subconscious controls the functions of your physical body, it causes your body to make almost the same changes and adjustments as it would as a result of actual physical exercise.

You actually can exercise in your imagination if you imagine it in vivid detail. However, you must see these things clearly in your imagination when you do them. You must get a good, vivid mental picture of the type of exercise you are doing.

If you wish, you may exercise in your imagination when you go to bed at night. It is better, though, if you do this exercise in the morning, and then you are ready for the day. This actually gives you more energy for the day. When you awaken every morning, just spend 15 minutes doing exercises in your imagination alone. Later on you'll find yourself actually doing these exercises in reality; but you can begin by exercising in your imagination alone.

Do this each morning of the week and see the results for yourself during the day. You'll feel more energetic, and be more active. You will get more done each and every day. Don't skip even one day—no matter what day it is. Take the time and exercise in your imagination for 15 minutes.

How to Practice in Your Imagination

As I have stated, psychologists have frequently experimented with a variety of methods to prove the benefits of practicing by imagination. I shall illustrate the proper manner in which practicing is done so *you* can practice in your imagination.

I have already given you illustrations about practicing golf and basketball in your imagination; but let me break down a little example here for the golfer. If you play golf—or any other sport or game in which you wish to improve your skill—you can certainly practice it in your imagination instead of doing it in reality.

A Game of Golf

Let's take one hole of golf and show you how to break it down in detail. You begin exactly as you would on the course. You mentally picture yourself walking up to the tee. You see yourself putting the tee in the ground and placing the ball on the tee. You see yourself selecting your club, and then taking your stance and practice swinging a couple of times.

Now you see yourself getting ready to hit the ball. You picture a perfect swing, a full and complete swing; perfect movements of the legs, arms, shoulder, hips—the whole body. Everything is in vivid detail. You see the ball sailing straight out, just as straight as can be, towards the green. You watch the ball land.

Then you see yourself getting into the cart and going down to the ball. Then you see yourself choosing a different club and going through the same thing. You see yourself hitting the ball up on the green. And you see yourself picking the putter, lining up your putt, taking your time, and so on.

Everything must be done exactly as it would be done in real life. If it takes you 15 minutes to play one hole of golf, then it should take you 15 minutes to play that hole of golf in your imagination in vivid detail. So just like exercising in your imagination, you must not skip over any parts of what you are doing. You must include as many details as you can; and each time you practice this way you find yourself including more and more details. You can do it over and over again until you are perfect at it. Thus results are yours.

Proving Your Own Powers

You can see now that imagination can help you get what you want, or it can prevent you from getting what you want. Either way—it's up to you. Used correctly for a good purpose, creative imagination creates what you desire.

Imagination is used extensively in hypnosis. But the hypnotist must make a clear picture for the subject to follow. If he doesn't, the subject fails to react in any way. By the same token, your subconscious responds to those things you imagine only when you imagine them in clear, vivid detail.

Test Your Imagination

Try a little test which will prove to you that YOU can create with your imagination. First, sit back in a straight back chair. Do not let your hands touch each other, but rest them on your legs. Don't cross your legs; just place your feet flat on the floor and relax.

Now close your eyes and imagine that to the right of you there is a little stool. And on that stool is a bucket of water. To the left of you is a burner of some kind—it can be a gas burner, an electric burner, or whatever—and on that burner there is another bucket of water. Now, picture this in detail. Get the buckets of water clearly in your mind before you continue.

Once you have these buckets of water clearly in your mind, picture the burner being turned on under the bucket to your left. Then visualize somebody dumping a lot of ice in the other bucket, the one that is sitting on the little stool to your right.

Now raise your left hand very slowly, move it over the water, and gradually immerse it in the water in the bucket on the burner. Be sure to wiggle your fingers and imagine you feel the water around them.

Then raise your right hand very slowly. Move it very slowly over to the other bucket and gradually immerse it in the icy water. Again wiggle your fingers and imagine you feel the cold water around them.

Now concentrate on two basic thoughts as you wiggle your fingers in these two buckets of water. First, the water in the bucket on the burner, in which you have placed your left hand, is getting warmer and warmer, and warmer and warmer. It is getting extremely warm.

The water in the bucket with the ice, in which you have placed your right hand, is getting colder and colder, colder and colder. It is getting very, very cold.

Concentrate only on the water in the two buckets. Feel how very hot the water is getting in the bucket on the burner and how icy cold the water is getting in the bucket with the ice. Take your time and concentrate on how hot the water is getting in one bucket and how icy cold it is getting in the other.

Another Word of Caution

Again a word of caution. Do not keep your hands in the buckets of water when one gets extremely hot and the other gets extremely cold, because your imagination is so powerful you could actually do yourself some harm. Many times I have seen people actually get burned from this type of test. Do not rationalize that the water isn't really there. If you created it in your mind, to your subconscious it's there.

This is another illustration of the truth of the statement that the subconscious cannot tell the difference between a real experience and one that you imagine in vivid detail. If you concentrate hard enough and imagine this experience in vivid enough detail, your subconscious accepts it and reacts to it as a real experience. And if you imagine that the water is hot enough and you leave your hand in it too long, your subconscious reacts in the same manner as though you had stuck your hand in hot water in reality—and creates a burn on that hand.

Hot Coin Test

Here's another test to prove the power of your imagination. And again I caution you not to continue the test too long.

Take a coin out of your pocket and place it in the palm of one hand. Then sit in a straight back chair and place your hands on your legs with palms up. Close your eyes now and imagine that the coin is getting warm. Take your time and concentrate only on that coin getting warmer and warmer, hotter and hotter. Continue concentrating on the coin getting hotter and hotter until it feels hot. Now, when the coin gets warm or hot, get rid of it immediately. Open your eyes and end the test. Again I want to warn you: many people have received blisters on the palm of their hand from holding the coin too long. So don't burn yourself. When the coin gets warm, quit.

Don't Underestimate the Power of Your Mind

All you want to do is prove to yourself *you* can create in your imagination. When the coin feels hot, get rid of it immediately. Do not underestimate the power of your mind. Some people have received sore hands by attempting to rationalize that the coin is not really hot. We know the coin is not really hot, but you have created a hot coin in your mind and fed this information to your subconscious which cannot tell the difference between something real and something imagined in vivid detail.

These tests will prove this fact to you. You can work out other tests for yourself and prove to yourself without any doubt that your imagination can create through your subconscious. But do so with caution. Never underestimate the power you have with your mind.

Don't Walk Too Far

I once had a student who underestimated the power of her mind and exercised too much in her imagination. She imagined taking long walks, and she enjoyed them so much that once she walked and walked for miles in her imagination.

The next day she was so sore she couldn't get out of bed. She found out the hard way that her mind was very powerful, and that her imagination, used in a creative way, was extremely powerful and through her subconscious it actually created a real effect. From then on she didn't walk quite so far.

Remember, your subconscious does not know the difference between what is real and what is imagined in vivid detail, so please proceed with care when doing these tests. By all means, though, find out for yourself that your imagination can create things through your subconscious so you can use this tool for a greater and more fulfilling future.

How to Imagine Yourself Successful

I want to give you an illustration, now, of how to use creative imagination in achieving a goal. Let's suppose you desire to be a business executive; this is your goal. Create a mental picture of you in your office, with the company name on the door and a name plate on the door showing your name and your executive position. Create a vivid mental picture of your office, seeing in your imagination every tiny detail you possibly can.

How big is your office? Is it square or long and narrow? Are the walls painted, or papered or panelled? What color are they? Is the woodwork painted or stained? What about the carpet: is it short nap or long, sculpted or shag? Is it solid color, tweed, patterned? How many windows are there in your office? Are they big windows or little windows? Do they get the morning sun or later afternoon sun? Are there drapes on the windows? Shades? Blinds? What view do you see from these windows in your office? In your imagination walk over to the windows and look out. What do you see?

How is your office furnished? What kind of desk do you have? Is it wood or metal? What color is it? What about the chair that you sit in: is it an overstuffed chair? Does it have a swivel base? What type, color, texture, and pattern of material is it upholstered in? What other furniture do you have? A credenza? Sofa? Coffee table? Lamp tables? Chairs? A bar? What style is the furniture? What wood is it made from? With what is it upholstered? What are the pictures on the walls? What kind of lighting does your office have? What do the lamps look like? What decorative appointments do you have in your office?

Ash trays, flower arrangements, plants, statues, cigarette boxes, or lighters? Are there magazines on the coffee table? Which magazines do you have? Are there bookshelves on the walls? What books are on the shelves?

What is on your desk? Files, literature, desk pen set, clock, radio, pictures? What does your secretary look like? Do you have a special hobby or have trophies or certificates of achievement in some skill which you display in your office? Does a beautiful aquarium or a special display of some sort add to the decor? Do you have piped-in music? Have you converted a small adjoining room into an exercise area?

Time and space do not permit me to continue itemizing detail, and I know you can add much more to this particular picture. But this is the type of detail you should include in your mental image of your goals and in the pictures you compose as visual aids for these goals. It is the vivid detail with which you create a mental image and compose your visual aid which gives power to the suggestion to your subconscious and causes it to react and materialize your goals for you. Your memory storehouse has endless detail recorded which you may draw upon, and you have unlimited imagination with which to imagine your goal.

An Aid to Creating Your Mental Image

Compose an actual detailed picture of your goal. When composing your picture, cut out a picture of your own face from a photograph and actually put yourself in the picture. YOU are the successful business executive and this is YOU in your office. Do this with every picture you compose as a visual aid for your goals.

When your picture is completed study it for 10 to 15 minutes every day and say to yourself, "This is me. This is what I am. This is what I have. I have already achieved it. It's already mine." Do this and success in achieving your goal is yours.

You can retrain your subconscious and get him to give you anything you want. He is the one that must materialize your desires. But remember, in order to practice, actually compose a real picture to concentrate on. If you can't find a picture showing your goal in detail, then draw one yourself. But do use a picture to look at and to concentrate on. Sit quietly and gaze at the picture for at least 10 to 15 minutes each ime. Think of nothing except that the person in the picture is you. You have already achieved your goal.

You can use your creative imagination as a tool to break bad habits and create new habits, to create a new, magnetic personality, to create dynamic self-confidence. In short, you can use the power of creative imagination to improve and better yourself in every area of your life.

How to Improve Your Social Poise

Perhaps you feel tense and ill at ease when meeting people for the first time. You find it difficult to take the initiative in making an acquaintance or starting a conversation.

Compose pictures of yourself greeting people, shaking hands with them, speaking to people, laughing and being relaxed, completely at ease. Study these pictures as often as possible. Soon you will feel the characteristics portrayed in your picture whenever you study it, and your subconscious will accept this mental experience or imagined experience as real. After several of these relaxed, pleasurable, and very successful social "experiences" in your imagination, you will have retrained your subconscious to create the same social poise in reality as it has experienced through your creative imagination.

How to Improve Your Image of "You"

Improve your own image of yourself through creative imagination by composing a mental picture of yourself exactly as you would like to be. Imagine yourself as being immaculately groomed, perfectly poised, relaxed, radiating friendliness and self-confidence. Imagine this new "you" until you feel and see every detail of this marvelous new image of "you" in your imagination. Once your subconscious becomes motivated by this experience, this new image of "you," you will be amazed and delighted at the changes which your subconscious will materialize.

How to Use Brainstorming

Most people today are familiar with the term "brainstorming," but too few of us use brainstorming as an approach to the solution of our own individual problems. Brainstorming, either individually or in groups, can be an effective means of employing imagination in forming a realistic appraisal of the value of any goal and the obstacles which must be overcome in reaching it; and it is a valuable aid in determining the most propitious means of reaching that goal.

Give Your Imagination Free Rein

Your imagination has no limitation unless you yourself place a limitation on it. Next time you are faced with a problem to which the answer has escaped you, apply the principles of brainstorming to secure the answer. First, make sure you understand what the problem is and have it clearly and concisely in your mind. Then don't try to think of an answer. Don't try to apply conscious effort or force an answer from your conscious mind. Give your imagination free rein to receive random and spontaneous ideas and thoughts about the problem, perhaps even in the form of mental pictures.

Don't Create and Criticize at the Same Time

As each idea or mental picture comes to you, jot down a brief description on a piece of paper. Don't try to keep all of these ideas in your mind because you want to leave your conscious mind completely free to receive additional ideas. So write each idea down as it is received.

And as the ideas come to you, don't attempt to analyze or

evaluate them. You can't be critical and creative at the same time. Some of the ideas may seem comical or ridiculous or absurd at the moment, but write each and every one down. These ideas that seem so completely lacking in merit or feasibility not only may spark other ideas, but very often they are the ones that hold the real answer. Remember that Jules Verne's idea about a submarine was "ridiculous" to millions of people—until it became a reality. Thomas Edison's ideas were "absurd"—until they became a reality. And the Wright Brothers' idea about a flying machine was certainly "comical"—until it became a reality and its impact was felt in almost every phase of our lives.

When you have compiled a lengthy list of ideas, then—and only then—review these ideas and analyze their feasibility. You will be amazed at how creative, how imaginative you really are when you remove the inhibitions, the limitations, you have placed on your imagination in the past.

Family Brainstorming

When seeking an answer in some area that concerns your family, involve the whole family in a brainstorming session. Don't hesitate to include the children in your brainstorming program and don't discard their ideas too hastily. Children are less inhibited in using their imaginations, and very frequently they can see the real core of a problem more readily because they are not encumbered by all the extraneous considerations which we adults sometimes have difficulty sorting our way through. Children are more spontaneous because they are not afraid of sounding foolish or absurd. So don't underrate the contribution your children can make to a brainstorming session on subjects which concern the whole family.

In addition to finding some surprisingly remarkable solutions to family problems, you will find that your whole family will have fun and actually enjoy these brainstorming sessions. And you will develop greater family unity when every member has an opportunity to express ideas and opinions and when he knows he is important and has a voice in the family.

Brainstorming Groups

Hold a brainstorming session with friends, both on subjects which concern you as an individual or subjects which may be of concern to the group. The ideas derived from such a session may be invaluable to you personally or to the group as a whole.

But let me emphasize two points again. In any brainstorming session—whether it involves you alone, your family, or any other group—make certain the problem is stated correctly and concisely and is understood by everyone. Secondly, lay down a strict rule—and enforce it rigidly—that no one may criticize any idea until after all ideas are written down. Then, and only then, will the ideas be criticized and evaluated.

Don't Re-create Your Failures

You have had both success experiences and failure experiences in your life. You were born successful and your success experiences greatly outnumber the failure experiences.

However, it is a very unfortunate trait in human nature that you react more strongly, more emotionally, to failure than to success. You most often forget your successes and dwell on your failures. You re-create your failures in your imagination again and again and again in minute detail until you actually feel again the disappointment, the frustration and the embarrassment which were evoked by the actual failure. You "experience" the failure again and again through your imagination—and your subconscious cannot tell the difference between real failure and failure that is imagined in vivid detail.

Through the lack of knowledge and understanding of the power of creative imagination and through its misuse, you literally turn one failure into five, ten, or even a hundred failure experiences—and your subconscious accepts each one as a real experience. It reacts to them as though they were reality, and it develops a habit of failure.

You Can Create Success from Any Failure

When you do fail at something, you can literally turn it into a success through the power of creative imagination. Take a critical look at the failure and analyze what caused it. Be objective and realistic and place the responsibility for the failure where it honestly belongs. Then never again re-create that failure in your imagination—never experience it again.

Instead, re-create the situation in your imagination; but with the new insight you have gained from analyzing the one failure, imagine yourself handling the situation, and solving the problem, in the light of your newly acquired knowledge, with complete success. Re-create the situation time and time again in your imagination; and each time you now handle the situation perfectly. You are completely successful in that particular situation.

You can turn that one failure experience into dozens of success experiences, each of which will be accepted by your subconscious as a true success experience. And if at some future time you are confronted with the same situation or a similar situation, your subconscious will react to these numerous success experiences you have created in your imagination by responding automatically and materializing the same success it has experienced so many times in your imagination.

Begin Now

In a very short while you will have proven to yourself the tremendous power of your own creative imagination and you will have retrained your subconscious to react to your desires and materialize them for you. Begin right now to use this tool to create your happiness and success—your future.

> "Most people are as happy as they make up their minds to be."

Abraham Lincoln

IMPORTANT POINTS TO RECALL

1. Create a mental picture of your goal as existing here and now.
2. Your subconscious cannot tell the difference between a real experience and one imagined in vivid detail. It reacts to both as a real experience.
3. Creative imagination is used in conjunction with repetition to recondition your subconscious.
4. Creative imagination is the most powerful tool you have at your command—either to get what you want in life, or to prevent you from getting what you want.
5. Creative imagination must be in vivid detail to be effective.
6. Fear is in vivid detail and is the strongest form of imagination which is not controlled. Fear creates that which is feared.
7. Because your subconscious cannot tell the difference between a real experience or one imagined in vivid detail, you can "practice" or do physical exercise in your imagination.
8. Brainstorming is an effective means of using your imagination.
9. Through creative imagination you can literally turn a failure experience into dozens of success experiences.

CHAPTER FIVE

How to Relax
and Concentrate

"Relaxation . . . it is the breathing time of day with
me."

Shakespeare

How many times today, or during the past week, have you
thought, "It would be so nice to be able to relax for just a few
minutes," or "I just can't ever seem to really relax"? How many
times have you asked the questions, "Who can relax at a time
like this?" "Who can relax with all this work to be done?"
"Who has time to relax?"

Well, the answer is YOU. You can relax, and you can and
must learn to relax and to concentrate if you want to get more
done and if you are to become a truly free, successful person.

How to Receive Many Benefits

This chapter teaches you a method of progressive relaxation
which I call "relaxation-concentration" which you can use to
achieve complete relaxation. But first I would like to discuss
with you the important benefits of mental and physical
relaxation and how very vital it is to your health and happiness
and to your future successes.

How to Vanquish the Monster "Stress"

Our mode of living today has created a monster of gigantic proportions which most of us find it impossible to do battle with—the monster called "stress." And the "fire" which this monster breathes is "tension." It is a very rare person today who has not succumbed to this tension and who has been able to remain mentally and physically relaxed and calm.

A Necessity for Overall Good Health

Medical science tells us that hypertension, or excess tension, very likely afflicts more people and is more destructive than all the diseases—such as cancer and heart trouble—which we lie awake at night worrying about. A great many of the "physical" ailments and complaints we have are actually caused by physical or mental tension—tension headaches, stomach ulcers, abdominal disorders, insomnia—to mention only a very few. Tension can and does make you ill; and relaxation is essential to overall good health.

If you are filled with tensions and anxieties, you cannot sleep well. And sound restful sleep is essential to good health and to mental and physical productivity.

Medical doctors state that if you are nervous or tense, it is more harmful to you to eat under those conditions than it would be to forego the meal entirely. Your body cannot work efficiently to process the food when you are tense and upset.

How to Restore Physical and Mental Energy

Tension depletes your physical and mental energy. You have to relax and allow your body to store energy so the energy will be available to expend during those times when tension is proper and necessary. When you are tense you burn excessive amounts of energy and you tire easily, both physically and mentally.

Professional athletes can tell you that undue tension limits the quality and endurance of their performance and causes fatigue. Artists will tell you that excess tension restricts their creativity and their ability to perform, whether they be painters, writers, or musicians.

How to Preserve Your Youthful Appearance

We live in a youth-oriented world, and millions of dollars are spent annually on creams, ointments, lotions, tonics and medications to keep us young and youthful looking. But we ignore the fact that relaxation is the best preservative of youth—youthfulness of mind, youthfulness of body, and youthfulness of face.

Those harsh vertical lines between the eyes and across the forehead, the crow's-feet at the corners of the eyes, the hard lines around the mouth—these are all placed there by frowning, squinting, anger—which are all forms of tension. You should learn to relax to preserve the vitality and suppleness of both your body and your mind and to keep your youthful appearance.

How to Remove Tension and Fear

Tension and fear walk hand in hand. It might be as difficult at times to answer the question of just which came first, the tension or the fear, as it is to answer the age-old question about the chicken or the egg. But fear does create tension; and as I showed you in past chapters, fear itself can create the very thing you fear when it is expressed in vivid imagination or creative wording. You must learn to relax. You must learn how to avoid the fears that create tensions which limit you and prevent your success.

How to Relax and Get More Done

Because money is essential in securing the necessities of everyday life, and because all of us but a very few must work at a job in order to make the money to pay for these necessities, our job, our work, is extremely important to us. And perverse creatures that we are, at those very times when it is the most advantageous for us to remain calm and relaxed so we can perform at the peak of our capabilities, we become the most tense and anxious. Too many of us create tensions and fears related to our work.

Tension in our work creates a vicious circle of misery. Tension undermines our self-confidence; and lack of self-confidence causes further tension. Tension impairs our judgment, and lack of confidence in our judgment creates more tension.

Tension limits both our mental and our manual dexterity and reduces our proficiency in our work. Tension is contagious and affects our co-workers. And tension certainly does not convey competency to our employers or employees. You must learn to relax before you can be efficient and productive in your work. When you are efficient and productive in the work you do, you are happy in your work, you enjoy it. And you must enjoy your work before you can be truly successful in it.

> "Unclamp, in a work, your intellectual and practical machinery and let it run free. The service it will do you will be twice as good."
>
> William James

Relaxation Is Contagious

Relaxation plays a vital part in developing and portraying a magnetic personality. A person who is nervous and tense does not convey confidence, enthusiasm, or happiness to others. Have you ever found yourself in the company of some person who was so keyed up, so tense and nervous, that it made you nervous just to be around him?

Tension is contagious. And so, thank heavens, is relaxation. If you are relaxed and content, people around you sense this and they "catch" some of this relaxation and contentment from you. They are relaxed in your company, they enjoy being with you. They have greater confidence in your judgment and your abilities.

Memory Recall Is Improved

Relaxation is important in order to learn concentration; and the ability to concentrate is one of the major functions of your mind and one of your greatest assets. Through relaxation and concentration you are able to learn anything faster and more easily; you have greater memory recall; you are able to pass tests on learned material with greater ease and accuracy; and you are a more effective and compelling speaker.

How to Establish Better Communication

You have learned of the power of creative imagination, and the tremendous part it plays in creating what you want in your life. But you must be able to concentrate in order to create vivid mental pictures. Through relaxation and concentration you have better communication with the subconscious and can gain more rapid mastery of it. This mastery of your subconscious is what enables you to create any success you desire. When you are the master, you are more receptive to new ideas and thoughts which come from without as well as those that come from within. You are able to secure answers from the subconscious and even from a Universal Force.

I do not wish to imply that there is no place in our lives for tension. There are times when it is proper and beneficial to be tense. If you are performing work that is difficult either physically or mentally, the energy and stimulation created by tension can be an asset, and tension is right and proper under such circumstances. But you have to learn to relax, to avoid tension, except when tension serves a specific and proper function.

Progressive Relaxation

Perhaps you are thinking, "This is all very good advice, but I just can't relax." Of course you can relax. You as a conscious mind are master of your subconscious; and your conscious mind and your subconscious together have complete control of the physical body.

In progressive relaxation—or relaxation-concentration, as I prefer to call it—you learn to relax and to concentrate; and you learn to use this concentration to control your physical body. Before giving you the proper wording, or "patter," for relaxation-concentration, I want to emphasize that when you use relaxation-concentration you must apply concentration on the parts of the body as they are mentioned. When reciting or mentally speaking the patter, at first take your time and speak very, very slowly, with long pauses between the different parts of the body as they are mentioned. Do not continue on until you actually feel a certain part of your body loosen up and relax, sometimes with a tingling sensation. It is very important that you give yourself plenty of time to really relax the portions of the body as they are mentioned before you continue on.

The Relaxation-Concentration Patter

Before using relaxation-concentration you should study the patter thoroughly and commit it to memory—word for word, if possible—for the most complete results. When you have learned the patter sufficiently well, make sure you are reclining or lying down in a safe, comfortable position and repeat the following to yourself:

> "I am going into very deep relaxation, letting all tension drain out of me completely, becoming loose and limp all over. Every muscle, every nerve, and every cell in my entire body is becoming completely relaxed.
>
> "It is easy to relax, to let all tension drain out of me completely. I feel so very wonderful in every way. Once any part of my body is relaxed, I do not allow that portion of my body to move a muscle.
>
> "Now I concentrate on the toes of my left foot. I think

only now of the toes of my left foot. I make them completely loose and limp.

"As I concentrate on the different parts of my body in this manner, I actually feel them with my mind. It's almost like my mind is touching the area I am concentrating on.

"I concentrate on the toes of my left foot as I loosen them so completely. I feel them as they relax. I feel the tension draining out of the toes of my left foot.

"Once any part of my body is relaxed, I do not allow it to move, unless any kind of emergency should arise, in which case I immediately terminate this relaxation and attend to the emergency as I normally would do. Or if I desire to terminate relaxation for any reason, I can do so immediately.

"If there is any emergency, I terminate my relaxation immediately and take care of the emergency as I normally would do. If for any reason I desire to terminate relaxation, I can do so immediately.

"I now create a moving wave of relaxation which moves very, very slowly into the different parts of my body as I concentrate on them.

"Now the toes of my left foot are completely relaxed, and this wave of relaxation is moving into the ball of my foot (pause), moving into the arch of my foot (pause), and slowly into the heel of my left foot (pause), and finally into the ankle of my left foot (pause), so that my entire left foot is completely and absolutely relaxed.

"Now this wave of relaxation moves slowly up my left leg. It moves into the calf of my leg (pause), into the large muscles behind the calf so that they are completely relaxed and I can feel them loosen up (pause), slowly moving into my left knee, deep within my knee and all around my kneecap (pause), becoming completely loose and limp all over so that my entire left foot and left leg, up to the knee, is completely loose and limp.

"This wave of relaxation moves on up into the large muscles of my thigh and they become completely loose and limp (pause), and very slowly this complete relaxation moves into my left hip (pause), so that my entire left foot, leg and hip are very loose and limp, completely loose and limp, and I shall not move a muscle in my left foot, leg or hip.

"As the wave of relaxation takes over, I feel the tension draining completely out of me. Everything is peaceful and enjoyable, so quiet and relaxing. I feel so wonderful. I am very calm and contented, very calm and very contented. All tension is draining out of me completely."

(You may feel a tingling sensation that sometimes appears as each part of your body relaxes. This is a perfectly normal, natural and pleasant sensation. It is only a sign that you are relaxing completely.)

"I now can feel how loose and limp my entire left leg, foot, and hip really are.

"The number one means my left leg, foot and hip are completely relaxed. The number one is a symbol that my entire left leg, foot and hip are completely relaxed." (You now also visualize the number "1" in your mind and visualize your left leg and foot and hip as being completely relaxed.)

"Now I concentrate on the toes of my right foot. I think only now of the toes of my right foot. I make them completely loose and limp.

"As I concentrate on the different parts of my body in this manner, I actually feel them with my mind. It's almost as if my mind is touching the area I am concentrating on.

"I concentrate on the toes of my right foot as I loosen them up completely. I feel them as they relax. I feel the tension draining out of the toes of my right foot.

"I now create a moving wave of relaxation which moves very, very slowly into the different parts of my body as I concentrate on them.

"Now the toes of my right foot are completely relaxed, and this wave of relaxation is moving into the ball of my foot (pause), moving into the arch of my foot (pause), and slowly into the heel of my right foot (pause), and finally into the ankle of my right foot (pause), so that my entire right foot is completely and absolutely relaxed.

"Now this wave of relaxation moves slowly up my right

leg. It moves into the calf of my leg (pause), into the large muscles behind the calf so that they are completely relaxed and I can feel them loosen up (pause), slowly moving into my right knee, deep within my knee and all around my kneecap (pause), becoming completely loose and limp all over so that my entire right foot and leg, up to the knee, is completely loose and limp.

"This wave of relaxation moves on up into the large muscles of my thigh and they become completely loose and limp (pause), and very slowly this complete relaxation moves into my right hip (pause), so that my entire right foot, leg and hip are very loose and limp, completely loose and limp, and I shall not move a muscle in my right foot, leg or hip.

"As the wave of relaxation takes over, I feel the tension draining completely out of me. Everything is peaceful and enjoyable, so quiet and relaxing. I feel so wonderful, I am very calm and contented, very calm and very contented. All tension is draining out of me completely.

"I now can feel how loose and limp my entire right leg, foot and hip really are.

"The number two means my right leg, foot and hip are completely relaxed. The number two is a symbol that my entire right leg, foot and hip are completely relaxed." (You now also visualize the number "2" in your mind and visualize your right leg, foot and hip as being completely relaxed.)

"Every muscle, every nerve and every cell is now completely relaxed from the tips of my toes clear up through my hips, and I am more calm and contented all the time. It feels so wonderful to really let go of all tension and relax completely. I am loose and limp from the tips of my toes to my hips."

(Perhaps you will feel a distinct heaviness or lightness in the parts of your body as you relax. This is perfectly normal and natural in every way. It is a sign you are relaxing completely.)

"I feel so wonderful. I feel so marvelous, so good, and any soreness or pain I may have had is leaving me now.

"Now I concentrate on the fingers of my left hand. I think only now of the fingers of my left hand. I make them completely loose and limp.

"I concentrate on the fingers of my left hand as I loosen them up completely. I feel them as they relax. I feel the tension draining out of the fingers of my left hand.

"I now create a moving wave of relaxation which moves very, very slowly into the different parts of my body as I concentrate on them.

"The tips of the fingers of my left hand are now completely relaxed and this wave of relaxation moves into the knuckles of the fingers of my left hand (pause), into the palm of my left hand (pause), into the back of my left hand (pause), and slowly into my wrist (pause), so that my entire hand is completely and absolutely relaxed.

"Now this wave of relaxation moves slowly up my left arm. It moves into my left forearm (pause), into my left elbow (pause), slowly into the large muscles of the upper arm (pause), and very slowly this complete relaxation moves deep into my left shoulder (pause), so that my entire left hand, arm and shoulder are very loose and limp, completely loose and limp, and I shall not move a muscle in my left hand, arm or shoulder.

"I now can feel how loose and limp my entire left hand, arm and shoulder really are.

"The number three means my left hand, arm and shoulder are completely relaxed. The number three is a symbol that my entire left hand, arm and shoulder are completely relaxed." (You now also visualize the number "3" in your mind and visualize your left hand, arm and shoulder as being completely relaxed.)

"Now I concentrate on the fingers of my right hand. I think only now of the fingers of my right hand. I make them completely loose and limp.

"I concentrate on the fingers of my right hand as I

loosen them up completely. I feel them as they relax. I feel the tension draining out of the fingers of my right hand.

"I now create a moving wave of relaxation which moves very slowly into the different parts of my body as I concentrate on them.

"The tips of the fingers of my right hand are now completely relaxed and this wave of relaxation moves into the knuckles of the fingers of my right hand (pause), into the palm of my right hand (pause), into the back of my right hand (pause), and slowly into my wrist (pause), so that my entire right hand is completely loose and absolutely relaxed.

"Now this wave of relaxation moves slowly up my right arm. It moves into my right forearm (pause), into my right elbow (pause), slowly into the large muscles of the upper arm (pause), and very slowly this complete relaxation moves deep into my right shoulder (pause), so that my entire right hand, arm and shoulder are very loose and limp, completely loose and limp, and I shall not move a muscle in my right hand, arm or shoulder.

"I now can feel how loose and limp my entire right hand, arm and shoulder really are.

"The number four means my right hand, arm and shoulder are completely relaxed. The number four is a symbol that my entire right hand, arm and shoulder are completely relaxed." (You now also visualize the number "4" in your mind and visualize your right hand, arm and shoulder as being completely relaxed.)

"I feel so wonderful. And now both my feet, legs, hips, and both my hands, arms and shoulders, are completely relaxed, loose and limp.

"Now I am relaxing the body proper itself. I think of the body as a unit—all the organs within my body as a single unit; and yet I am able to feel each and every part loosen up completely. Every single muscle, nerve and cell is now relaxing completely.

"Now I take a deep breath, a very deep breath. I inhale as deeply as I can; and I hold the air in my lungs for a second or two and then let the air out very slowly. As I let this air out completely, I feel my body relax all over. I feel all tension draining out of my body completely.

"Now I take another deep breath, a very deep breath. I inhale as deeply as I can; and I hold the air in my lungs for a second or two and then let the air out very slowly. As I let this air out completely, I feel my body relax all over. And now all tension is almost gone from my body.

"And now I take a third deep breath, a very deep breath. I inhale as deeply as I can; and I hold the air in my lungs for a second or two and then let the air out very slowly. As I let this air out completely, I feel any remaining tension leave my body completely. Every single muscle, nerve, and cell in my body proper is now relaxed completely and all tension is gone.

"I feel so very pleasant, so calm and very contented. It is so good to slow down.

"Now I am relaxing my head and neck. I concentrate on my scalp, each and every area of my scalp, and relax each part of it, making it completely loose and limp. I loosen it up completely.

"I now start a wave of relaxation, very gently and very slowly moving down and deep within from the scalp, moving down my left side. This wave of relaxation moves down into my left ear (pause), and down into the left side of my neck (pause), so that the relaxation there meets the relaxation in my left shoulder.

"And now this wave of relaxation moves down the right side of my head, very gently and slowly, moving down and deep within from the scalp. This wave of relaxation moves down into my right ear (pause), and slowly down into the right side of my neck (pause), to where this relaxation joins with the relaxation of my right shoulder.

"And now I start this wave of relaxation down into my forehead from my scalp, very gently and very slowly moving down into my eyes (pause), all around my eyes relaxing, behind my eyes relaxing, over and under my eyes relaxing completely, so that every muscle, every nerve and every cell is completely relaxed.

"And this wave of relaxation now moves slowly and

gently down into my nose (pause), into my cheeks (pause), into my lips (pause), slowly down into my chin (pause), and very slowly moving from my chin into my throat area (pause), so that it is completely relaxed, loose and limp.

"Now that my chin is completely relaxed, loose and limp, my teeth part a little.

"And now I concentrate on the back of my skull and the back of my neck, deep, deep within the base of my skull and deep within my spine and neck muscles. Very, very slowly I loosen this area completely, and make it completely loose and limp.

"If at any time I have a slight headache, I can remove it entirely by relaxing this area completely, by concentrating and letting go of all tension.

"The number five means my entire body, from the tips of my toes to the top of my scalp, is completely and totally relaxed. The number five is a symbol that all tension is gone entirely, and every nerve, every muscle, and every cell in my entire being is completely loose and limp, completely relaxed." (You now also visualize the number "5" in your mind and visualize your entire being as completely relaxed, completely and absolutely loose and limp all over, completely and totally relaxed.)

(If you desire to go deeper into relaxation, take more deep breaths as before, and you go deeper and deeper into relaxation.)

When you first begin to practice relaxation-concentration speak the patter very slowly. Concentrate on each area as you come to it in the patter and keep your mind focused on each particular area until it is completely relaxed. Make sure each area is completely relaxed before you go on to the next area.

Then every time you do this relaxation-concentration you should go through the patter a little faster, because each time you will relax faster.

How to Relax at the Count of Five

The numbers 1 through 5 which you spoke and visualized as

each part of your body relaxed now become the symbols for relaxing that particular area of your body. Each time you do relaxation-concentration you reinforce the power of suggestion of these symbols so at some time in the future all you have to do is think, "1, relax," and your entire left foot, leg and hip are completely relaxed. "2, relax," and your entire right foot, leg and hip are completely relaxed; and so on.

This count from 1 through 5 is never effective unless you are in a safe comfortable position and desire to relax and use this count for the specific purpose of relaxing. At all other times, counting from 1 through 5 has no effect upon you whatsoever and you do not respond to it in any way.

YOU Can Relax

Everybody can learn to relax. Remember, you as a conscious mind are the master of your subconscious. And your conscious mind and your subconscious together have complete control of the physical body.

If you are the person who says you are too busy, too rushed, to be able to afford ten or fifteen minutes now and then to relax, you are the person who can least afford not to take the time to relax. If some problem or question arises in your work and the answer eludes you, or if you feel yourself tensing up under work pressures, take a ten or fifteen minute break, find a quiet place where you can relax in comfort and safety and put yourself into relaxation. You will be amazed at the results.

If you arrive home from a hard day's work full of tension and irritability, find a quiet spot in the house and put yourself into relaxation. By relaxing completely for these few minutes, you'll find the attitude and the disposition and the energy to enjoy your family and your home. And you'll certainly be a better husband or wife and a better parent to your children.

Before going out socially or having guests in your home, put yourself into relaxation. You will be a more enjoyable guest, a more congenial host, and a more delightful companion for having done so.

Soon you will find some very interesting and wonderful

changes taking place in your life. You will allow tension to remain within you only when it is proper and beneficial and serves a specific purpose. At all other times you will be able to remove all tension and relax completely, thereby becoming a healthier, happier, more contented person. Other people will welcome the opportunity to work with you or to enjoy your company in a social setting.

Relaxation Is Half the Battle

Relaxation is not the cure-all for all of life's problems, but when you can approach these problems in a relaxed manner you have won half the battle. You are able to exercise better judgment, utilize more of your talents, think and act more creatively, and receive answers to these problems more accurately and more promptly through better communication with your subconscious. And you will have taken another giant step towards becoming a truly free, successful individual.

IMPORTANT POINTS TO RECALL

1. Relaxation is essential to the truly free, successful person.
2. Tension limits your power of judgment, your abilities, your memory recall, and your communication with your subconscious.
3. You use relaxation-concentration only when you are reclining or lying down in a safe, comfortable position.
4. The relaxation-concentration patter should be recited very slowly when you first begin to practice, and then should be spoken a little more rapidly each time it is used.
5. Relaxation can always be terminated immediately in the event of any emergency or if you have a desire to terminate relaxation for any reason.
6. The numbers 1 through 5 become symbols for the relaxation of the various parts of the body. Through repeated use of relaxation-concentration and the reinforcement of the sug-

gestion concerning these symbols, you will eventually be able to relax your entire being completely by merely thinking, "1, 2, 3, 4, 5."

7. As you speak the numbers 1 through 5, you must also visualize the numbers and visualize that particular area of your body as being completely relaxed.

CHAPTER SIX

Opening Lines
of Communication

In Chapter One, "Understanding the Relationship Between Success and You," you learned the importance of developing communication between your conscious mind and your subconscious.

- Your subconscious is a serving mechanism and it is your subconscious which must materialize your desires for you on this plane of existence. Therefore, you must be able to communicate your desires to your subconscious.

- Your subconscious is your "memory bank" and you have to open the line of communication between your conscious mind and your subconscious in order to improve your memory recall.

- You should retrain your subconscious and remove false beliefs which have been programmed into it through past conditioning so you can eliminate the conflicts between the conscious mind and the subconscious which limit you and which can lead to a mental problem. You must be able to communicate with your subconscious in order to retrain it and remove these false beliefs.

Self-Hypnosis

Self-hypnosis is an excellent means of opening a line of communication with your subconscious which enables you to communicate desires and suggestions to your subconscious and retrain it by removing false ideas and creating new habits.

In the past, hypnosis has been considered by many people to be something mystical, faintly tinged with the occult, or merely a trick of deception contrived by a performer with the same cunning and "sleight of hand"—and deserving of the same incredulity—as the magician who historically wears a long flowing cape and saws ladies in half. Even today many people view hypnotism with skepticism, incomprehension and misunderstanding, or fear.

A Natural and Marvelous Phenomenon

In reality, there is nothing mystical about hypnosis. There is no deception involved. And although there is such a power in hypnosis that its use should always be treated with respect and sound judgment, there is nothing about it that should cause fear. Hypnosis is simply a natural and marvelous phenomenon wherein the subconscious is rendered more suggestible and direct communication with the subconscious is made possible.

A Popular Misconception

The traditional use of the word "sleep" as an induction into hypnosis and the reference to a hypnotized person as being in the "sleeping" state are probably responsible for the most popular misconception and the greatest reticence people have concerning hypnosis.

The words "sleep" and "wake up" are used only as a matter of expedience because the word "sleep" holds connotations of dreaminess, detachment, wandering, and relaxation of the conscious mind; and "awake" is construed as meaning mentally alert and perceptive.

A person in hypnosis is not asleep in the literal sense of the word, and he in no way loses consciousness with his conscious mind. His subconscious is simply induced into a state of detachment so it is possible to communicate more directly with it. He consciously hears and understands every word that is spoken to him and retains his ability to think and reason. He can accept or reject any suggestion given to his subconscious. Generally, if his conscious mind rejects any suggestion, his subconscious will not react to it.

Every Hypnotic Subject Really Hypnotizes Himself

A person in hypnosis retains absolute and complete control of himself at all times; and his will cannot be subjugated to the will of anyone else through hypnosis alone.

The power and effect which a hypnotist's words have over his subject is possible only because the hypnotized subject *believes* he is under the spell of the hypnotist and because he *accepts* the suggestions given to him. Experiments have proven beyond doubt that when a subject who is going to be hypnotized is told that he and he alone has absolute control at all times, the hypnotist can do nothing without the consent of the subject.

In addition, experiments have proven beyond any question at all that when a subject is told that he himself has absolute control, it is more difficult to put him into hypnosis. This is why every hypnotic subject *really hypnotizes himself*. He can be hypnotized, but only by himself. If another person is going to hypnotize him, the subject must permit the hypnotist to be the guide; and when he is aware he is being hypnotized, the subject won't do anything that he doesn't want to do.

Upon awakening from light or medium hypnosis you can recall every word that was spoken and every action you performed during hypnosis. In deep hypnosis the conscious mind may wander or daydream; and because of this a person may or may not recall what was said or what took place while he was in hypnosis—unless suggestions are given to recall everything or to recall nothing. In a sense, it is similar to recalling a dream. The ability to recall dreams varies from person to person, and in any particular person the ability to recall varies at different times.

It is possible that while under deep hypnosis you may be given the suggestion that upon leaving the state of hypnosis you will recall nothing that has taken place. Again your conscious mind makes the decision to accept or reject the suggestion before passing it on to your subconscious. If you accept the suggestion, upon leaving the hypnotic state you will recall nothing that has taken place—but only if your conscious mind desires to accept the suggestion.

In hypnotherapy the therapist usually does not advise the patient that he has the ability to either accept or reject the suggestion that he will not recall what has taken place under hypnosis. Generally the patient has complete confidence in his therapist and complies with such suggestions without question. But even under such conditions there are instances when the patient does not accept the suggestion and recalls everything that happened—even when instructed not to.

Suggestions May Be Rejected

On occasion, when a patient has been undergoing hypnotherapy for some time and has the ability to go into deep hypnosis, the therapist may wish to regress the patient back to some particular period of time in the patient's life. The therapist knows that some incident occurred during that time which has created problems for the patient; and he wishes to regress the patient to that time period in order to obtain information about the incident which will enable him to help the patient to overcome his problem.

However, the patient may consciously be unwilling to reveal the details of this incident to the therapist. This being the case, he rejects the suggestion given him under hypnosis and refuses to relive that particular period of time. He may reject the therapist's suggestion and actually skip over that incident during repeated sessions of hypnosis until some future time when he has more confidence in his therapist or a better understanding of the importance of recalling that specific period and relating the details of the incident to his therapist.

The patient has consciously refused to allow his subconscious to recall and reveal a given time in his life. This is just one instance proving that a subject, even in very deep hypnosis, is still capable of reasoning with his conscious mind and rejecting the hypnotist's suggestions.

Two Kinds of Hypnosis

There are basically two kinds of hypnosis: hetero-hypnosis, in which one individual hypnotizes another; and auto-hypnosis, or self-hypnosis, in which an individual hypnotizes himself. In reality, even in hetero-hypnosis, a person hypnotizes himself because he and he alone, through his conscious mind, makes the decision to accept hypnotic suggestions when he is aware he is being hypnotized. If he does not desire to be hypnotized and rejects the suggestions, he cannot be hypnotized even by the most experienced hypnotist.

A Powerful Aid

Our concern here is with self-hypnosis as a powerful aid in implementing the tools you are going to use to create a new, successful "you."

As I have pointed out, your conscious mind makes decisions and formulates your desires into words and mental pictures which it communicates to your subconscious; and your subconscious alone has the ability to materialize your desires on this plane of existence. Therefore, anything you can do to facilitate this communication between your conscious mind and your subconscious intensifies the impact your suggestions have on the subconscious and accelerates the speed with which your subconscious will respond in materializing your desires.

You Can Learn More Rapidly

In ancient times the Greeks had what they called "sleep temples" where young men from wealthy or influential families went to study. In these sleep temples the young men were taught how to go into very deep relaxation; and they remained in this deep relaxation while the teacher gave them their lessons and instructed them. When the teacher had finished giving them their material for that day, he would awaken them and they would return to their homes. We recognize that the results from this type of learning were superior to any other method of teaching we know of even today.

When you go into hypnosis your body is actually more relaxed than at any other time or any other way. Circulation is better, your nerves are relaxed. All tension is gone. This is why you feel so wonderful when you awaken from hypnosis.

And it is important you understand that through hypnosis you can get your words or thoughts, your desires, across to your subconscious much faster, much better, much stronger, than any other way known. Once you understand hypnosis you can more easily understand this. It's only a matter of you being the master and getting your subconscious to react and respond to your suggestions.

There Are Many Benefits

There are many additional benefits to be derived from the use of self-hypnosis which I should mention very briefly. Through self-hypnosis you can achieve more complete mental and physical relaxation; and this relaxation is in itself an invaluable asset in this fast-paced world we live in. You can sleep better, deeper and more soundly. Both of these abilities enhance your physical and mental health.

Through the use of self-hypnosis you can improve your power of concentration and your memory recall. You can break unwanted habits more easily. You can remove soreness and pain. You can deaden the jaw for dental work or deaden the whole body for surgery without any anesthetic at all. And most important, as I have already pointed out, you can learn faster than any other way known to man.

Test Your Degree of Susceptibility

Everyone has a different degree of susceptibility to hypnosis because everyone has a different degree of susceptibility to suggestion. At this point I would like to give you a few very simple tests you may use to determine your own personal degree of susceptibility to self-hypnosis.

Before performing any of the tests you should be completely awake and alert. Also, several of the tests require you to be seated in a safe, comfortable position before you begin.

How to Terminate All Tests

Also before beginning the tests you should be aware of the proper means by which the tests should be terminated. First, in the event of any emergency, any effect of the test or any response you may have to the test would be immediately terminated, and you would take care of the emergency as you ordinarily would do.

When you wish voluntarily to end the test you use a key word or a key picture in your mind; and this key word or mental picture must be something which is completely un- related to the test, yourself, or hypnosis. For example, you might use the word "monument" because it is a word that is certainly unrelated to you or any test or purpose to which you would generally apply self-hypnosis.

When you wish to terminate the following tests of your susceptibility to hypnosis, or when you wish to terminate any test of any kind that is related to self-hypnosis, speak the word "monument" out loud or picture a monument (perhaps the Washington Monument) in your mind. It is necessary to either form the mental picture of your key monument or speak the word "monument" so that should you perform a test where you are unable to speak and cannot say the word "monument" out loud, you can then create a mental picture of your key monument and thus end the test.

As an illustration, when you begin to use self-hypnosis you may wish to perform simple tests. One such test might be that while you are in a state of self-hypnosis you may give yourself the suggestion that when you awaken you are unable to speak until you picture your key monument. When you awaken from a hypnotic state during which you have given yourself such a suggestion, you will think you are able to speak and you will try repeatedly to say something. But because you have given yourself the suggestion under hypnosis that you cannot speak until you picture your key monument, you will actually be unable to speak. Then you can simply create a mental picture of your key monument, which will terminate the test; and you will then be able to speak.

Another simple test you can perform is to suggest to yourself while under self-hypnosis that upon awakening you will be unable to get up from the chair until you speak the word "monument" or picture your key monument. Then when you awaken from hypnosis you think you are able to get up and you try to get up from the chair but you cannot—until you speak the word "monument" out loud or until you picture your key monument.

As I said earlier, you may use any key word or picture you choose, so long as it is completely unrelated to yourself, hypnosis, or the test itself. I use the word "monument" only for the purposes of illustration in the tests shown here.

Always use your key word or key mental picture to terminate any test. At first, of course, some people would be able to terminate any test or any hypnotic suggestion without using a key word or key picture; but it is best right from the start to begin conditioning your subconscious to respond to your key. So be consistent. Terminate every test—and tests only—by speaking aloud the word "monument" or visualizing a monument, such as the Washington Monument, or any other key word or picture you have chosen, and you will have taken a very important step in training your subconscious.

Test Number One

For the first test, sit back in a reclining chair, or any chair where you are comfortable and in a safe position. Hold your arms straight out in front of you with the palm of one hand turned up and the palm of the other hand facing down. Be sure that your arms are straight.

Now close your eyes. Concentrate and imagine in as much detail as possible that someone is putting a very heavy book in the palm of the hand that is turned up and you are holding the book up in the air. Then imagine, again as vividly as possible, that someone is tying a string around the wrist of the hand with the palm facing down and on the end of the string is a large balloon which is pulling your hand and arm up into the air.

Now suggest to yourself that the book is getting heavier and heavier and pushing the one arm down. And suggest to yourself that the balloon is getting lighter and lighter and pulling the other arm higher and higher—one arm being pushed down and the other being pulled up.

Now imagine that another heavy book is put on top of that other book, and the books are extremely heavy. And imagine that another balloon is tied to the other wrist, pulling that arm even higher.

The arm holding the books is going down lower and lower; and the other arm is lifted higher and higher and higher by the balloons. The arm holding the books is going down lower and lower and lower; and the other arm is lifted higher and higher and higher by the balloons.

Imagine all of this in vivid detail. Feel how heavy the books are. Picture how big they are and how much pressure they place on your arm, causing it to fall lower and lower and lower. Feel the pull of the balloons, how they rise higher and higher and higher towards the ceiling, pulling your arm up, up, up.

Then open your eyes and see what kind of results you have

achieved. If you have used your imagination in vivid detail, and if you have not tried to hurry through the test but have given yourself ample time for the one arm to rise with the balloons and the other one to fall under the weight of the books, generally when you open your eyes you will find that the hand that was holding the books is way down low, and the one around which the balloons were tied is held up higher in the air.

After you have opened your eyes and seen the results you achieved from this first test, speak the word "monument" aloud, or picture a monument, such as the Washington Monument, terminating the test, and let your arms fall naturally into your lap.

You have completed the first test, and if one arm was perceivably higher and the other lower, you have determined that you are susceptible to hypnosis to some degree.

Test Number Two

Let us go on to another test. This test is similar to the first one, except that you clasp your hands in your lap. So again sit back and relax and clasp your hands tightly together in your lap. Place your feet flat on the floor.

Now close your eyes and imagine that your hands are now a vise, the kind of vise used on a workbench to hold objects while they are being worked on. Imagine your hands as being such a vise and imagine you are screwing the vise up tighter and tighter, tighter and tighter. Keep repeating this slowly to yourself and imagine this vise is getting tighter and tighter, tighter and tighter, tighter and tighter. Your hands are coming together even tighter and tighter, tightening up, coming together tighter and tighter, screwing together like a vise. They are coming together tighter and tighter, tighter and tighter.

You will reach a point where your fingers will feel fixed and rigid. When you reach this point and your hands are very tight together, then imagine they are glued together, they are stuck fast, glued fast together, stuck together, and you cannot get them apart. There is no way you can get them apart. They are stuck fast. Glued together. Stuck fast, glued together. They are made together as one. You cannot get them apart.

(The exception, of course, would be that in the event of an emergency of any kind you would immediately take your hands apart and attend to the emergency. Otherwise, your key word or key picture is the only way of cancelling the test.)

Your hands are glued together. They are stuck fast and you cannot get them apart. There is no way you can get them apart except in the event of an emergency or until you speak the word "monument" or picture a monument. Your hands are like a vise; and you have screwed the vise up extremely tight and locked it into position. You have locked it tightly into position, so tight that your hands are as if welded together.

The vise is very tight now, and it is stuck fast, locked into position. You cannot get your hands apart no matter how hard you try, no matter what you say or think, except in the event of an emergency, or until you speak the word "monument" or picture a monument.

Continue to concentrate solely on your hands and imagine in as much vivid detail as possible that your hands are indeed glued together, your hands are a vise, and the vise has been closed and locked so tightly your hands are welded together. You cannot separate them or pull them apart until you speak the word "monument" or picture a monument.

Remember, you must suggest to yourself that there is no other way for you to get your hands apart, you cannot get them apart any other way except as I have indicated.

Now try to get your hands apart. You will find it is impossible to do, or quite difficult at the very least. You have again proven you are susceptible to hypnosis. Now speak the word "monument" out loud or picture a monument and terminate the test and take your hands apart.

There are many such tests you can work with. Some tests, however, require skill or the presence of another person to observe or be present for safety's sake. In performing any test, be certain to take all necessary precautions for your own physical safety, such as being seated in a safe, comfortable position.

Also, whenever you are performing these tests, continue giving yourself the suggestions for a long enough period of time for you to feel the effects.

Inductions into Hypnosis

The "tools" we have discussed in previous chapters are all used in some way in different forms of induction into hypnosis. For example, we use repetition to gain the attention of the subconscious and to maintain our communication with it. We use visual imagery when we use the induction in which a person sits in a chair and uses his eyes to gaze at one spot or one object in the room with the thought that his eyelids are getting so very heavy that he cannot keep them open.

The methods of induction into hypnosis are many and varied. One of the methods of induction which is best known because of its simplicity is called progressive relaxation. I refer to it as "relaxation-concentration." Part of this induction involves the use of the "relaxation-concentration patter" which you learned in the previous chapter. This induction technique is very effective for almost everyone.

Key Words and Key Suggestions

We use many key words and key suggestions in self-hypnosis; and we use the key word "sleep" repeated three times in our induction. As I explained before, we use the expressions "sleep" and "wake up" although you are not actually asleep when you are in hypnosis and can "awaken" at any time you desire.

If the telephone rings while you are in self-hypnosis you can simply get up and answer the telephone if you want to. It is better, however, to condition your subconscious properly by using the key "wake up" or "awaken" before you jump up to answer the phone.

If somebody comes to the door while you are in hypnosis and you desire to answer the door, again you can simply say or think "wake up" or "awaken" and then get up and answer the door. You will be completely and fully awake with no adverse effects at all. You may feel slow and sluggish immediately upon getting up, but this is only because you were gaining relaxation which was needed. After considerable practice in self-hypnosis, you will get up immediately feeling full of pep and energy.

When your subconscious has an opportunity to relax—and it has this opportunity under self-hypnosis—it usually takes advantage of it. And if you always use the key "wake up" or "awaken" to terminate a hypnotic state, or even relaxation, it helps you overcome this sluggish feeling you may have in the beginning immediately upon getting up, as well as providing better conditioning for your subconscious.

Provisional Meanings of the Word "Sleep"

The key word "sleep" which is repeated three times as a part of the induction into self-hypnosis has certain provisional meanings which are very important:

1. The key word "sleep" repeated three times by you puts you into hypnosis ONLY when you desire to enter self-hypnosis. At all other times the word "sleep" has no effect on you and you do not respond to it in any way.
2. The use of the key word "sleep" repeated three times is effective in inducing hypnosis ONLY when you are in a safe, comfortable position where you cannot fall or injure yourself.
3. Every time you go into hypnosis, you go deeper and faster than at any previous time until you reach the deepest possible depth of hypnosis.
4. You always awaken from hypnosis immediately in the event of any emergency.
5. At any time you awaken from hypnosis or a normal and natural sleep you feel extremely wonderful all over, free and clear, full of pep and energy.

6. You always awaken from hypnosis at the time you have predetermined or at the time you desire to awaken while in hypnosis.

All six of the above-mentioned conditions are summed up in the one word "sleep" repeated three times.

While you are learning self-hypnosis, always practice while reclining or lying down. If at a later time you wish to enter self-hypnosis while you are sitting up, have your head supported in some fashion so it will not fall sideways or downward.

And remember that the key word "sleep" for entering self-hypnosis has no effect upon you unless it is your desire to enter into self-hypnosis and you are in a safe, comfortable position. You will never enter into self-hypnosis when it is dangerous for you to do so, but only when you can go into self-hypnosis with absolute safety.

The Relaxation-Concentration Technique

When you use the relaxation-concentration technique as an induction into self-hypnosis, remember to apply concentration on each part of the body as you mention or think of it in the patter. When you first practice self-hypnosis, take your time and repeat the patter very, very slowly mentally with long pauses between the different parts of the body as they are mentioned. Do not continue on until you actually feel each part of your body loosen up and relax—sometimes with a tingling sensation as I mentioned before. It is most important that you give yourself plenty of time to really relax the parts of your body as they are mentioned before you continue on with the patter. Then each time you practice self-hypnosis you may mentally recite the patter a little faster. Each time, you relax more quickly and you enter hypnosis much more rapidly and more deeply than at any time before.

When learning the relaxation-concentration patter you assigned the numbers 1 through 5 as symbols representing the relaxation of various parts of the body until at the count of 5 your entire body is completely relaxed. In self-hypnosis, the word "sleep" repeated three times replaces the count of 1 through 5. With continued practice, in time you will be able to merely repeat the word "sleep" three times and go immediately into self-hypnosis.

An Induction

Assuming you have now committed the relaxation-concentration patter to memory and are ready to go into self-hypnosis, make sure you are reclining or lying down in a safe, comfortable position, and we will begin now with the induction into self-hypnosis:

"Sleep—I close my eyes and begin to relax. Both feet, legs and hips are now completely relaxed.

"Sleep—I breathe deeply two times; and now both hands, arms and shoulders are completely relaxed.

"Sleep—My entire being is now completely relaxed. I go into a very deep relaxation, letting all tensions drain out of me completely.

"If I desire to go deeper into hypnosis, I take more deep breaths as before, and I go deeper and deeper into hypnosis, deeper and deeper asleep."

(At this point continue on as follows while in self-hypnosis, repeating each of the following paragraphs twice.)

"At any time in the future when I desire to enter self-hypnosis, and when I am in a safe, comfortable position, when I repeat the word 'sleep' three times I immediately go into very deep hypnosis, very deep asleep." (Repeat.)

"At any other time, the word 'sleep' will have no effect whatsoever upon me." (Repeat.)

"Each and every time I desire to enter self-hypnosis, and when I am in a safe, comfortable position, when I repeat the word 'sleep' three times I go deeper into hypnosis than at any time before, until I reach the deepest possible depth of hypnosis." (Repeat.)

"Whenever I desire to awaken from self-hypnosis, I count backwards from five to one. I awaken gradually with each count. At the time I reach 'One,' I immediately open my eyes and am then completely awake. I feel good all over, free and clear all over, no soreness or pain of any kind; full of pep and energy. I feel better than I have ever felt before in my life." (Repeat.)

"I always awaken immediately in the event of any emergency of any kind." (Repeat.)

"Whenever I desire to go into self-hypnosis and when I am in a safe, comfortable position, I simply repeat the word "sleep" three times and I immediately go into hypnosis, much faster and much deeper than at any time before, until I reach the deepest possible depth of hypnosis." (Repeat.)

(It is at this point in self-hypnosis when you may mentally recite your creatively worded suggestion for whatever goal you are working on at the time. Also, in a later chapter you will learn how to summarize your worded suggestion and your mental picture of your goal into one key word or letter which then becomes the symbol for that goal until it is achieved. At this point in self-hypnosis you may also use that key word or letter.)

(After you have given yourself these worded suggestions you may continue quietly in self-hypnosis until you awaken at a predetermined time or you may terminate hypnosis at this time. You should always terminate self-hypnosis by using the following patter:)

"I now count backwards from five to one. I awaken gradually with each count, and at the time I reach "One" I open my eyes and I am completely awake. Every time I awaken from self-hypnosis I feel wonderful all over, free and clear.

"Five ... four ... three ... two ... ONE. My eyes open and I am awake. I feel wonderful all over, free and clear, full of pep and energy."

(At some future time after you have practiced self-hypnosis consistently and reinforced your waking suggestion, you can awaken by simply counting backwards from five to one. On the count of "One" you will immediately be completely awake, feeling wonderful all over, free and clear, full of pep and energy.)

Other Lines of Communication

As I have said, hypnosis is one of the most effective ways of communicating suggestions to your subconscious.

There are also several excellent ways of opening lines of communication with your subconscious so you can receive information from him, or from a Universal Force, by means of your subconscious.

How to Use the Pendulum

One excellent means of communicating with your subconscious involves using the movements of an object which is held so it dangles and forms a pendulum. The pendulum may be any small object such as a key or ring or pendant which is suspended by a chain or thread eight to ten inches long.

To use the pendulum, sit in a relaxed, comfortable position at a table or desk, with both feet flat on the floor. Be sure you are seated so you are comfortable and not tense in any way. Place one arm comfortably on the table or desk top. Hold the thread or chain of the pendulum between the thumb and forefinger of the other hand, resting your elbow on the table or desk top and allowing the pendulum to dangle freely.

As you will see in Figure 2, there are four basic movements which can be made by the pendulum: clockwise circle, counter-clockwise circle, back and forth horizontally in front of you, and back and forth vertically (towards you and away from you). Each of the four movements should be assigned one of the following four meanings: "Yes," "No," "I don't know," and "I refuse to answer the question at this time."

This last meaning or answer may sound rather presumptuous or rebellious on the part of your subconscious. But there are instances in which it would be improper or not to your benefit

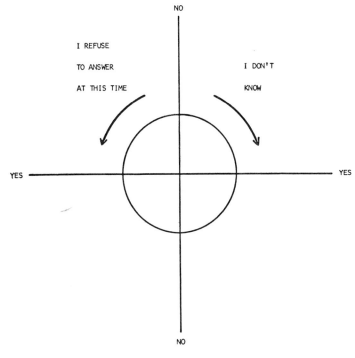

Figure 2

to know the answer to a particular question, and your subconscious will answer through the pendulum in this manner.

Now that you are properly seated and holding the pendulum between the thumb and forefinger in the correct manner, address your subconscious directly and ask: "Which way will the pendulum move to answer 'Yes' to questions?" After you have asked the question, remain quiet, gaze at the pendulum, and wait for it to move. It will generally move in a matter of seconds.

Do not make any conscious movements or try in any way to influence the movements of the pendulum in a particular direction. Your subconscious needs no conscious effort or guidance to control the muscles involved in breathing, or sneezing, or opening and closing your eyes. The subconscious coordinates and controls these movements without your conscious guidance, and it will coordinate and control the muscles and their movements which are necessary to move the pendulum in the proper direction.

After the pendulum has moved and indicated which direction it will move to indicate "Yes" answers, on a separate piece of paper make a sketch of Figure 2 and indicate on your sketch the movement the pendulum will make for "Yes" answers.

Now pose the same questions for the other three possible answers: "No," "I don't know," and "I refuse to answer the question at this time," and indicate the movement for each answer on your sketch.

Then again addressing your subconscious directly, ask him if he will answer any questions for you at this time. If the answer to that question is affirmative, ask him if he will answer questions about the particular subject you wish to question him about. If the answer is again affirmative, you may proceed to ask questions related to that subject. At times you may find that your subconscious is willing to answer questions on one subject but will refuse to answer questions on another at that particular time. So always ask him if he will answer questions on a specific subject.

Remember that the answers you receive through the pendulum come from your subconscious, and they may conflict with your conscious opinion. It may take some time to properly attune yourself to communicating with your subconscious through the pendulum, but once you are attuned, the pendulum can be a valuable assistant in communicating with your subconscious—especially in uncovering things which happened in your earlier years.

Keep in mind that your subconscious does not have the ability to reason, and therefore he cannot answer questions which require reasoning, such as "Would I," "Could I," "Should I," etc. But if you state your questions accurately and explicitly, and if you are a little patient in developing this line of communication, you can receive many answers from your subconscious, or from a Universal Force through your subconscious, by using the pendulum.

Automatic Writing

Another very effective way of gaining information from the

subconscious is through automatic writing, although it may take some time to learn to use it.

If you wish to attempt to develop an ability to communicate with your subconscious in this manner, seat yourself comfortably at a desk or table with a large writing pad in front of you; or, preferably, write on a lap board to give your hand freer movement.

Place a soft pencil or a ball-point pen in your hand and suggest to your subconscious that it take control of the muscles of the hand and fingers and write without conscious guidance. Then ask questions of your subconscious.

With automatic writing you are usually unaware of what you are writing. You may occupy your conscious mind with other matters such as reading, daydreaming, or even talking to another person while the hand is writing. It is even possible for a few people who have developed exceptional proficiency in automatic writing to read material on one subject, write with the right hand on a second subject, and write with the left hand on a third topic.

When writing automatically, at first the words are usually run together, and the letters are frequently poorly formed, making it very difficult to interpret at times. Most often the writing is done slowly, but in some instances, the hand may seem to race across the writing pad.

Also, the writing may be very cryptic. For example, the words "to," "too," and "two," may be indicated simply by the figure 2, or the word "before" may be written as "b 4." Also, the writing may be backwards, upside down, mirror writing, or a combination of all three. But with practice, generally in time the writing gets clearer and is written in a proper form.

Doodling is one form of automatic writing and many doodlers can learn automatic writing easily with some practice. Doodles frequently have meanings which can be interpreted just as dreams can be interpreted.

We have now discussed several ways in which you may communicate more directly with your subconscious. So open these lines of communication and strengthen them. They are very important tools in conveying suggestions to your subconscious and in receiving answers from both your subconscious and a higher source or power.

IMPORTANT POINTS TO RECALL

1. Lines of communication between your conscious mind and the subconscious are extremely important because: You must communicate your desires to your subconscious so it can materialize them for you; your subconscious is your "memory bank"; you must retrain your subconscious to eliminate false beliefs, conflicts and harmful habits.
2. Hypnosis is simply a natural and marvelous phenomenon wherein the subconscious is more suggestible and more direct communication with it is possible, and self-hypnosis is an excellent means of opening a line of communication with your subconscious.
3. A person in hypnosis is neither unconscious or asleep. He consciously hears and understands every word spoken to him and retains his ability to think and reason.
4. A person who is hypnotized can accept or reject any suggestion.
5. Every hypnotic subject really hypnotizes himself.
6. Through self-hypnosis you can achieve more complete mental and physical relaxation; sleep better, deeper, and more soundly; improve your power of concentration; improve your memory recall; break unwanted habits; remove soreness and pain; and learn faster than any other way known to man.
7. Everyone has a different degree of susceptibility to hypnosis.
8. All tests to determine your degree of susceptibility, or any tests performed while using self-hypnosis, should be terminated by a key word or key mental picture which is completely unrelated to the test, yourself, or hypnosis.
9. In the event of any emergency, self-hypnosis is immediately terminated, or any effect of a test or any response you may have to a test is immediately terminated.

10. The key word "sleep" repeated three times as part of the induction has certain provisional meanings: 1. You go into self-hypnosis ONLY when you desire to; and 2. ONLY when you are in a safe, comfortable position; 3. each time you go in deeper and faster; 4. you always awaken immediately in the event of any emergency; 5. every time you awaken from self-hypnosis you feel wonderful, free and clear; and 6. you always awaken at the time you have predetermined or at the time you desire to awaken.
11. You awaken from self-hypnosis by counting backwards from five to one. You awaken gradually with each count, and on the count of "One" you are wide awake.
12. The pendulum and automatic writing are excellent ways of receiving information from your subconscious.

CHAPTER SEVEN

Drawing Upon
Hidden Powers

You are often told how very small and insignificant a part your life plays in the world, how infinitesimal you are in the overall picture of the universe.

Now, in terms of physical proportion this is certainly true. But in the sense that it implies you are insignificant or powerless, or that your very existence is inconsequential, it most definitely is not true. You are a very important part in the scheme of things. And although your physical stature may be small as far as the amount of space it occupies in the universe, you are an extremely important part of life. You have access to the greatest power, the greatest force, the greatest intelligence in the universe.

If you have not considered yourself to be very happy, very successful, very important, or very powerful in the past, you may have reason to doubt the truthfulness of what I have just said. That is only because in the past you have not known how to be your own master. You have not known about the tools which you already possess or known how to use them. You have not known how to reach and use the unlimited power available to you. You have not known of the unending help you have in creating any success you desire.

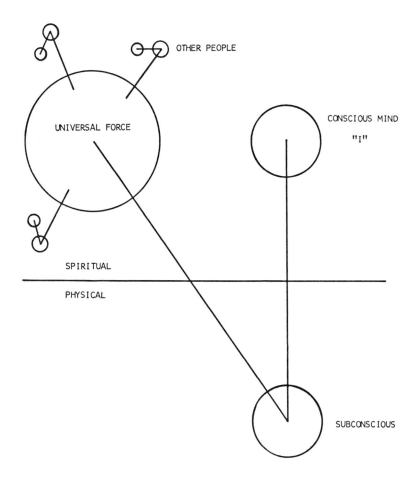

UNIVERSAL FORCE

OTHER PEOPLE

CONSCIOUS MIND

"I"

SPIRITUAL

PHYSICAL

SUBCONSCIOUS

Figure 3

A Sixth Sense

When a man enjoys spectacular success or exercises almost miraculous judgment in his business dealings, it is sometimes said of him, "He seems to have a sixth sense when it comes to business matters." When an individual makes an important decision which later appears to have been made with some remarkable or mysterious insight, the comment may be made, "It's almost as if he had some sixth sense about it."

Many great inventions, many world-molding decisions, have

been born of "inspiration," "hunches," and "intuition." But from where do these inspirations, hunches, and intuition emanate? Is a "sixth sense" some special gift with which only a chosen few are blessed?

A Universal Force

The sixth sense is the "sense" or line of communication through which every individual can communicate with a Universal Force or power. The information from this Universal Force or power is received in the form of ideas and thoughts which flash into the conscious mind—and these ideas and thoughts are sometimes called inspirations or hunches.

Everyone has equal access to this Universal Force, but there are few who are aware of its existence and who recognize and act upon the information received from it. Once you become aware of this Universal Force, once you learn how to open your lines of communication with it, once you learn to recognize the information and guidance received from it, then there is no end to the strength you can draw upon. There is no limit to the knowledge you have available to you.

There Is One Mind Common to All

Emerson said, "There is one mind common to all individual men." And this is a reference to this Universal Force and the fact that there is one gigantic Universal Intelligence common to all men or available to all men.

Ideas Are in the Air

Edison said ideas are in the air and if he had not discovered them someone else would have. Again notice the reference that knowledge is already there and all you have to do is learn how to reach it. The "air" that Edison mentioned is another reference to this Universal Force or Intelligence.

You Have Access to Knowledge

In his book *Psycho-Cybernetics* (Prentice-Hall, Inc.), Dr. Maxwell Maltz relates: "Dr. J. B. Rhine, head of Duke University's parapsychology laboratory, has proven experimentally that man has access to knowledge, facts, and ideas other than his own individual memory or stored information from learning or experience. Telepathy, clairvoyance, and precognition have all been established by scientific laboratory experiments. Dr. Rhine said, in words to this effect, that there is a capacity to acquire knowledge that transcends the sensory functions."

In other words, knowledge is available from sources other than through the five senses. The only thing that keeps you from gaining or using this knowledge is that you don't recognize its existence or know how to reach it.

You Have Access to Power

Dr. Maltz continued on to say, "Every human being has access to a power far greater than himself." In other words, everyone has access to a Universal Force, power, intelligence or knowledge.

There is absolutely nothing prerequisite to communicating with this Universal Force and receiving this knowledge and guidance that you do not have within you. There is no magic or mystery, no supernatural power required. This knowledge is available to everyone. This power is available to all, and it is merely waiting for you to put it to use.

The Power of Belief

Generally the only thing which keeps you from gaining or using knowledge available to you from the Universal Force is that you don't have the faith required to get at this knowledge. And this brings us again to that very important word "belief."

I discussed "belief" earlier when I pointed out to you that your beliefs, like anything else, were acquired during your lifetime and were created by your past conditioning. I think you now have an understanding of how powerful false beliefs have been in limiting your happiness and your success. So let's consider now how powerful belief can be in *creating* happiness and success.

You Have Unlimited Power

There is *unlimited* power in believing. In the Bible we are told, "Verily I say unto you that whosoever shall say unto this mountain be thou removed and be thou cast into the sea and shall not doubt in his heart but shall believe, those things which he sayeth shall come to pass and he shall have whatsoever he sayeth." Faith or belief can move mountains—but only when there are no doubts of any kind; only when there is not the slightest hint of a doubt; when all questions are removed.

An Impossible Feat

I have on the wall of my office a picture of an Indian walking on hot coals which were measured by members of the National Geographic Society Expedition at 1,328 degrees Fahrenheit. This Indian man was examined by members of the expedition both before and after he walked across the hot coals and he had no burns or sores of any kind on his feet.

Science tells us that this is impossible, that 1,328 degrees would char his feet to cinders, burning all the flesh completely away from his feet and legs; it would burn him to ashes. And yet this man walked across hot coals measured at 1,328 degrees Fahrenheit and showed no effects at all, not even a blister.

How could this man do something which science tells us is absolutely impossible? Through faith. Because he believed. He believed that he could walk across the hot coals without harm or injury to himself.

I can't help but wonder how much we could accomplish if we were taught this limitless faith from childhood. If we were taught to believe in ourselves and our tremendous powers and abilities as we grew up, how great and how masterful we could be.

In the Biblical story of Jesus walking on the water, how different is that "Miracle" from the miracle of the man walking on the hot coals? Again science tells us that such a thing as walking on water is utterly impossible. But Jesus believed he could walk on the water—and he did.

Belief Heals

In Matthew 9:22 we read the story where Jesus said to the woman, "Daughter, be of good comfort. Thy faith has made thee whole. And the woman was made whole from that hour." Another "miracle"? Jesus said that her own faith, her own belief, had healed her.

And again in Matthew 9:28 Jesus asked, "Believe ye that I am able to do this?" And then he said, "According to your faith be it unto you," again pointing out that it was this person's own individual faith that healed him.

Cultivate Your Own Belief

We live in a world of "instant" beverages, "instant" foods, "instant" cities—almost "instant" everything. And I regret I cannot offer you "instant" belief. Belief, however, is something which must be learned and nourished by each of us.

But I do hope I have been able to plant some "seeds" of belief which you will cultivate: Belief in the power of the tools which you possess and with which you can create any success you desire; belief that you as a conscious mind are master of yourself and your future; and belief in the existence of a Universal Force or power which offers you guidance and assistance in everything you do *if* you will only remove the barriers which past conditioning and the ignorance of science and society have placed between your conscious mind and this Universal Force.

Don't Interfere

When you occupy your conscious mind in trying to use willpower, trying to make elaborate plans towards accomplishing your goal, consciously trying to force some action, your conscious mind is too preoccupied to receive ideas and guidance from the Universal Force.

When you have a desire or a goal, use the tools of creative imagination, creative wording, acting-image when it is called for, and repetition. Then don't interfere by using further conscious effort. Relax and let this higher power, this Universal Force, formulate and implement the plan for materializing your goal. It can certainly do a far better job than you can with your conscious mind alone.

"Sleep On It"

You have heard people say, "Well, I'll sleep on it and let you know," or "Sometimes it helps to sleep on it for a while." There is more value in "sleeping on it" than you may have supposed in the past. Many great men and women have stated that a beautiful lyric, a haunting melody, the outline of a literary masterpiece, or the last piece of a scientific jigsaw puzzle, was born from inspiration received while sleeping or as a result of sleeping on a problem.

Your subconscious never sleeps. It continues to coordinate and control your physical functions—your heart beats and your lungs take in and expel air—even while your conscious mind sleeps. And while you sleep, your subconscious continues to record all suggestions or sense impressions; and it does so without the interference of your conscious mind.

When you have a problem or you need the answer to a

question, pose the problem or the question to your subconscious before going to sleep at night and expect an answer when you awaken the following morning. Convey this question to your subconscious clearly by verbally speaking the question or stating the problem in detail. And then sleep on it and expect an answer the next morning.

As a beginner, you may not receive these answers right away. Very few people ever get results immediately. Like all other lines of communication between you and your subconscious, this one must also be strengthened and perfected. But if you continue to "sleep on it" and give your subconscious time to react to this new means of communication, you soon see the results. And shortly you become very much aware that your problems or your questions are being worked on by a higher power and that they are being answered much faster than you as an individual could obtain the answers with your conscious mind alone.

You Are a Spiritual Being

We are all conscious beings. This is our identity. We are spiritual. We are only using our physical being. It is like temporary housing for our conscious mind.

As I said before, the you that you call "I" is the conscious mind. Although it is spiritual and cannot be located or seen, we know it is there and we know what it is capable of—and through the strength, power and intelligence it draws from the Universal Force, it is capable of anything.

In Matthew 6:25 we are told, "Therefore I say unto you take no thought for your life, what ye shall eat or what ye shall drink nor yet for your body what ye shall put on. Is not life more than meat?" This scripture tells us that true life is more than meat, more than our physical body. True life is the spiritual you, your conscious mind.

And in Matthew 6:19, we read: "Lay not up for yourselves treasures upon earth where moth and rust doth corrupt and where thieves break through and steal, but lay up for yourselves treasures in heaven where neither moth nor rust doth corrupt and where thieves do not break through nor steal. For where your treasure is, there will your heart be also." Surely we wouldn't be admonished not to lay up treasures on earth if this were the only existence we would know. Nor would we be told to lay up treasures in heaven if our earthly death, the death of our physical bodies, were a final and absolute end for our total being. We know that the spiritual part of man, his conscious mind, does not experience death. Your conscious mind, which cannot die, is your true "life." It is the real "you."

In Luke 12:4 we are told, "And I say unto you my friends be not afraid of them that kill the body and after that have no more they can do," which in effect is stating that we are spiritual now, the true "us" is spiritual, our true life now. The body can be killed, but "you" cannot experience death.

Have No Fears for the Physical Body

Once you know your conscious mind is your true life rather than your physical being, then you realize that your conscious mind must surely be the master of your whole being and your whole life.

When you accept this truth, and when you accept that your conscious mind has unlimited power it can draw from this Universal Force, then you remove many of the fears you have been conditioned to have concerning the health, welfare, and appeasement of the physical part of you, your body.

Remove All Limitations

Where have you placed your limitations? You are the master of your life, master of your own fate—and you have no limitations unless you yourself place them there. You are master of anything if you believe without doubt.

The only thing which can hold you down is your own lack of faith that you can do something. So many people have limited themselves to their own small worlds, their own small existence. The life lived by the average individual is hypnotic. Not one person in a million feels the freedom to live what he inwardly feels he should live. He has come under the spell of society's opinion of himself, and it is this opinion that he obeys rather than obeying the law of his own being.

In this respect and to this degree he is living under a hypnotic spell. He lives under the delusion he is a mere human being living in a merely material world; and he only hopes to escape it when he dies and goes to what he calls heaven. But you must begin now to remove all boundaries, all limitations, and begin opening up your mind to new ideas and new thoughts.

Take Time to Learn

These results you are looking for will not come to you overnight. It takes time for you to learn and understand and to develop your powers and the ability to use these tools to the point where they are effective rapidly. But each and every day you will find yourself believing more and more strongly in the power of these tools, and then you will discover yourself using them daily.

Never let doubt into your life for it will always defeat you. Believe you are a conscious mind, a spiritual being, and that you are really master of your subconscious, your physical being.

> "Great men are they who see that spiritual is stronger than any material force, that thoughts rule the world."
>
> Ralph Waldo Emerson

You Can Attract or Repel

You have the power to attract anything and everything you want. But you must be careful because you also have the power to repel these very same things. Yes, you have the power to attract or repel any and all things. This is the power which enables some men to climb to great heights and keep on going up and up and up; and yet at the same time, it is the power which keeps others down at the bottom.

This great power is always present within you. It is always working in one of two directions—either for you or against you. In other words, you are either putting it to use or it is putting you to use. You either put this power to use for your own goals or you will discover it is using you for somebody else's goals.

Once you know the secrets of this great power within you, you will be the master forever and never again the slave—either to your subconscious, your past conditioning, or the desires of others. You can direct the course of your life, rather than following the desires of others. Now, as I said before, this great power is always there and it's always working. If you don't use it, someone else will. Therefore, you may be doing things to fulfill the desires or goals of others instead of your own desires and goals.

A New Adventure in Living

You have embarked on a new and exciting adventure in living. You are discovering many things which you never realized before. You are meeting, for the first time, the most important person in the world—and that person is "you." When you do meet yourself honestly and completely you will discover life's secrets and the tremendous power which lies within you now.

IMPORTANT POINTS TO RECALL

1. It has been proven experimentally that man has access to knowledge, facts and ideas other than his own individual memory or stored information from learning or experience. There is a capacity to acquire knowledge which transcends the sensory functions.

2. Everyone has equal access to this Universal Force once they learn how to communicate with it.

3. There is great power in belief. Scientifically impossible feats can be performed through belief.

4. You should cultivate belief that you as a conscious mind are master of yourself and your future; belief in the power of the tools which you possess; and belief in the existence of a Universal Force or power which offers you guidance and assistance.

5. Your subconscious seems to be the link between your conscious mind and this Universal Force.

6. When you have a desire or goal, you should use the tools of creative imagination, creative wording, acting-image when it is called for, and repetition. Then don't interfere by using further conscious effort.

7. Your subconscious never sleeps; and sleeping on a problem or question is an effective way to receive answers from the subconscious and the Universal Force.

8. You are master of your own existence, your own life. Through the power of the tools you have and the guidance of the Universal Force, you can be anything, do anything, and create any success you desire.

9. The only thing which can hold you back or defeat you is your own lack of belief.

CHAPTER EIGHT

Your Starring Role

I think at some moment in each of our lives we have a secret desire to be an actor or actress. And all of us at different times play little "roles" or act a particular "part" in our imagination or in real life.

The ability to act a part, to assume for a time a character or personality other than our own, to imagine and create an image in our mind, is a talent which is unique in human beings. And now you will use this very unique talent to change your habits, your beliefs, and your future. You are going to act the part of the successful person you wish to be. You are going to act out the successful accomplishments you wish to achieve.

A Key to Success

You realize by now that the keys to being a free, self-controlled, successful individual are right with you. And you now know that one of those very important keys is "belief."

In Chapter One, "Understanding the Relationship Between Success and You," you became more aware of exactly what your present thinking, habits and beliefs are. And in the subsequent chapters you discovered how some of those beliefs and habits are limiting you and holding you back from being completely successful.

Actions vs. Beliefs

Your actions almost always conform with your beliefs because you generally act like the person you think you are. Your beliefs govern you to such an extent that they can determine whether you will be successful or be a failure in your future.

If you believe you are a failure, you set out to prove you are a failure. If you believe you are energetic, you try to prove you are an energetic person. If you believe you can't learn something, you generally prove to yourself that you cannot learn it. On the other hand, if you believe you are extremely successful, you set out to prove you are successful. If you believe you can learn anything at all and learn it well, you generally prove you can learn anything and everything you have a desire to learn.

There are success-type personalities and there are failure-type personalities; happiness-type personalities and sad-type personalities; health-type personalities and sick-type personalities— all determined, to a major degree, by their beliefs.

What You Think of Yourself

But notice I said your beliefs are what you *think* of yourself. They are not necessarily the true abilities you have today. They are not necessarily the true "you." And since you usually conform to your own beliefs about yourself, you can see the importance of knowing exactly what your beliefs are and knowing how to change the ones which are false and hold you back.

Above all, you should learn to believe in yourself. Not false beliefs, but true beliefs based on your true abilities and powers.

Beliefs Are Acquired

No one is born with a particular belief. You acquire your

beliefs from living, from experiencing, from past conditioning. You learn to believe in your family, in your friends, in your religion, in your profession, and in yourself. You also learn to disbelieve in these very same things.

I assure you that your beliefs, like your habits and skills, can be changed. You can eliminate bad habits and acquire new ones. You can eliminate false beliefs, or beliefs which limit you. You can acquire new beliefs where you are truly unlimited. And you can acquire these new habits and beliefs just as easily as you acquired the ability to drive a car, swim, play tennis, or even to feed yourself.

You are never too old or too young to change your beliefs. Failures can become successes, and shy and inhibited people can become happy, free individuals—when they change their beliefs and their habits.

A New "Tool"

If you are to develop new beliefs and habits you must begin to act differently. In the past you have probably tried many ways to change your habits, with very few results. So now I would like to show you how to use this unique ability man has of being able to "act a part" to create an acting-image, which is another major tool. Acting-image is a very effective tool in making any change you wish to make in your present habits and beliefs.

Why Acting-Image Is Effective

First, let's review for a moment some of the things you have learned earlier in this book so you can understand just why acting-image is so effective.

You learned of the purpose and function of your subconscious. You now understand how it is conditioned and how it responds or reacts to that conditioning. Never forget that your subconscious acts like a computer and it responds in the way you condition it to respond or in the way you program it to respond. And you can change that programming. But *you* must be the one who does the programming.

You have learned how to use creative wording and creative imagination in vivid detail, together with repetition. You know that experimental and clinical psychologists have proven that the subconscious cannot tell the difference between a real experience or one which you create in your own imagination in vivid detail; and when you repeatedly create an experience in vivid detail in your imagination, your subconscious reacts to that imagined experience in the same manner as it reacts to a real experience.

You also know that when you use creative wording together with repetition, your subconscious accepts your creatively worded suggestion as a fact and it reacts to materialize what you say. And you must also remember that your subconscious reacts according to the literal meaning of the words and not what you *intend* them to mean.

Adding a New Dimension

To the basic principles of the tools creative wording, creative imagination and repetition you now add a new dimension—acting the part. Now you have an extremely powerful tool called "acting-image."

As I have said before, your beliefs define the boundaries of your actions, your future accomplishments and your successes. Now you can change any beliefs which are false or limiting and you can expand those boundaries by acting the part of the person you want to be.

Simple Logic

The logic is very simple:

- Your subconscious reacts according to how it is conditioned to react.

- Your subconscious is conditioned by experiencing, by suggestions.
- Your subconscious cannot tell the difference between real experiences or those experiences you "create" in vivid detail.
- When you use your acting-image to portray a new characteristic, a certain personality, through repetition your subconscious reacts to this experience.
- Your subconscious develops new habits to conform with these experiences, this new conditioning.
- The new habits become part of "you" and you make them part of your own self-image.
- You develop a new belief about yourself.

Your Past "Performances"

You have used this tool, acting-image, countless times in your life without being aware of it. For example, as very young children most of us identify with someone driving a car. We pretend or imagine we are driving a car. We imitate mother and dad by sitting behind the wheel and touching the various controls, and we "play-act" the motions of driving the car. Our having acted from such a tender age the part of someone driving a car is responsible in part for the ease with which most of us are able to master the actual art of driving.

When we reach the point where we formally begin driving instruction, we again "act the part." We get in the car and go through all the correct motions—a little awkwardly at first, perhaps—but still imitating what we have observed others do, still acting a part.

Through repeated experiences we refine and perfect our performance. Everything required in the operation of the car becomes automatic, a natural reaction, a habit. Through practice, through experiencing, our acting-image becomes our true-image, a natural part of our true self.

A Basic Example

Learning to walk is an even more basic example of the use of this tool, acting-image. When you learned to walk as a child you didn't just get up and walk and run immediately. You got up and walked and fell. You got up and walked again and you fell again. You imitated the movements of people around you who did walk and you acted the part of someone who could walk.

You practiced over and over again; and you kept at it until you could walk without falling. Today you walk automatically, without any conscious effort. It is second nature to you now, an automatic reaction.

A Major Influence

A major portion of your personal characteristics—your physical actions and gestures, your personality—has been created as a result of your identification, either consciously or unconsciously, with someone who possessed those characteristics. And through identification, your acting-image, you have acted the part of that characteristic or trait until it became a part of "you."

You Have Acted Blindly

But in the past you have not even been aware that you were acting a part and you have been completely unaware of the effect it has had upon you. You have used this tool blindly and acquired many undesirable habits and beliefs.

Now you can begin to use this tool to remove those habits and beliefs you have acquired which are detrimental to you and which limit your success. And you can use this tool to become the person you truly want to be. You can condition your subconscious to any new personality trait or habit, and a new belief, in the same way, and with as little effort, as you learned to walk or drive a car.

Creating Your Acting-Image

You must practice this new experience you desire to make a part of "you" over and over again by acting the part in vivid detail in order for your subconscious to create a new habit. But eventually it will react automatically in real life situations in the same way you condition it to react through acting the part, and this new habit will truly become a natural part of the "new you."

Just as creative imagination and creative wording must be used in vivid detail and must express your goal as being "here and now," you must be a good actor and play the part well.

A Script

A good actor has a script which he studies. Then he practices the script in his imagination and in the words he speaks. A good actor actually "lives" the part. Now, he doesn't do this the first time, does he? When he picks up the script for the first time, he simply reads it. He certainly can't act the part brilliantly right off the bat. But after considerable practice and considerable time spent in going over and over the script and imagining the scene, the set-up on the stages and so forth, then he becomes adept at acting that particular part.

In effect, during his performance a good actor becomes that person he is portraying or acting the part of because he has conditioned himself to be that person. Once he plays that part and once it is completed, he goes on to the next role.

If I could give you one magical wand which would open the door to a more successful life, that magic wand would be acting-image, or acting the part of the person you wish to become. But you must prepare the script. You must practice

your script in your imagination and in the words you speak.
And you must be a good actor.

Everybody can be an actor, but your script will be different
from the script for a T.V. program. Your script will go a great
deal deeper and have far more meaning because the role you
write into your script, the character you portray, will be the
person *you want to be.*

Project Yourself into Your Role

When an actor plays a part repeatedly in a T.V. serial, or a
Broadway play, or even throughout the filming of a movie, even
though it is just a script, when he is acting the part he actually
becomes the person he is acting out. He learns the part so well
and projects himself into the character so completely he can
actually feel and think as the character would. The role he is
playing becomes almost second nature to him and it is easy for
him to act that part.

I think everyone has at some time seen a performance in
which an actor or actress played the part so well that he or she
almost seemed to become that person, where even his physical
appearance seemed to change. One example would be Joanne
Woodward's magnificent performance in the movie "Three
Faces of Eve," in which she portrayed three very different
personalities. She projected herself into the character, into the
personality she was playing, so completely that as she adopted
the manner of speech, the posture, the facial expressions of the
different personalities, her physical appearance actually seemed
to change.

And we have all seen actors who at different points in their
professional careers played completely different types of roles.
At an early stage in his career Dick Powell played a song-and-
dance man in many movies. Later in his career he changed to
tough-guy detective roles. And he was very successful in both
characterizations. James Cagney was equally convincing as a
vicious killer or "the good guy."

Your Unlimited Imagination

True, we have not all developed our powers of imagination or our dramatic skills to the same fine point as the great actors and actresses of the entertainment world. But we do all have unlimited imagination—unless we ourselves place a limitation on it. And you have a distinct advantage in that you are not going to act the part of a character or personality which someone else has defined. You are going to write your own script; you are going to create your own character, your own role. You are going to produce and direct your own performance. And you are going to be your own critic.

If you want to achieve harmony in the family, then you have to act as if there is harmony in the family. If you want to achieve confidence, then you have to act confident. If you want to be successful, you must experience success, and your acting-image must portray success. You have to practice being this successful person. You are, in a sense, playing a role, you are acting the part. But in time your subconscious reacts automatically to this experience you have created by acting the part. Then you no longer have to act the part because it actually becomes a part of you, part of your new self-image. Your beliefs will have been changed and you will believe yourself to be that successful person you set out to become. You are that person.

A Successful Acting-Image

Let's create an imaginary salesman, whom I shall name Ralph, and let's examine for a moment how acting-image might be used to benefit you in your profession.

If Ralph wants to be successful as a dynamic salesman, he must certainly act like a dynamic salesman, and his first step is to write a script of the role he is going to portray. Because all of Ralph's thinking and habits and beliefs have been created by past conditioning, his belief as to what constitutes a successful salesman was also created by past conditioning with those outstanding salesmen with whom he has been associated.

Since it is extremely unusual for any one person to be a paragon of perfection in even one isolated area, Ralph's definition of the perfect salesman is a composite of different impressions from many experiences involving various people. Therefore, this total character Ralph develops in his script, this role of the perfect salesman Ralph wants to be, should be a composite of characteristics from different people.

So first Ralph thinks about the successful salesmen he has known or been associated with; and he analyzes these successful men to determine the characteristics, the personal habits and the work habits which contributed most to their success. Then Ralph writes a detailed script about a dynamic, successful salesman who possesses all the qualities and assets which he has determined a successful, dynamic salesman must have. Each individual quality or habit is a *short-range goal*. The total character (the dynamic, successful salesman Ralph wants to be at this time) is his *long-range goal*.

First Short-Range Goal

The outstanding quality Ralph found in Bill, who is very successful, is that Bill always seems so alert and full of energy in the morning, full of enthusiasm and ready to face the day. Ralph knows that a successful salesman is on the job early in the morning and is physically and mentally alert before his first appointment. Ralph, however, has a tendency to catch just five more winks every morning and doesn't really "come alive" until after his third cup of coffee.

Ralph talked to Bill and asked him what the secret of his "instant energy" was. Bill told him that he had formed a habit of exercising for 15 minutes every morning, and he believed it was this exercise, followed by a brisk shower, which gave him that extra boost every day. So in his script Ralph writes the part of Bill who arises immediately upon hearing the alarm every morning, exercises for 15 minutes, and showers to get himself physically active and moving.

Second Short-Range Goal

The outstanding thing Ralph has noticed in Tom, who is tremendously successful, is that he "looks" so successful. So in Ralph's script "Tom" pays strict attention to his personal cleanliness and dresses each day in clean, neat clothing that is suitable for his profession. He is immaculately groomed and he looks every bit the successful businessman.

Third Short-Range Goal

In the past Ralph has been very impressed with the manner his associate Jim has in his relationships with his clients. Ralph knows that to become the successful salesman he wants to be he must come in contact with people and he must greet them well, just as Jim does. He must inspire their confidence in his ability and honesty and he must be aggressive without being overbearing. And Ralph now writes the part of Jim into his script. In the script "Jim" is honest with his clients and his employer. He does not hem and haw or speak evasively. He knows that one of the keys to success is the ability to speak out clearly in a sincere, forthright, forceful manner. And Ralph imbues the character "Jim" in his script with all these qualities.

Fourth Short-Range Goal

Continuing on with his script, Ralph includes the part of "Joe" who knows his product thoroughly and is always prepared with the required documents and tools which are necessary to make a sale.

Fifth Short-Range Goal

Ralph also includes in his script the role of "Sam" who

knows his means of transportation is vital to his work and therefore gives it the attention it requires to be in good operating condition and present a good appearance at all times.

A Dress Rehearsal

And Ralph continues writing his script, step by step, including every detail which goes into the make-up of this successful, dynamic salesman he desires to be. When his script is finally complete he is ready to begin working towards his first short-range goal by acting the part of "Bill." He reads and rereads the script until he has memorized the character, until he understands the role he is to play and can act the part without having the script in front of him. And then he is ready for his dress rehearsal.

(It is very important that you always keep in mind that you are playing a role, you are acting the part of the person who possesses the attribute you wish to acquire. By playing the part of a person completely separate from yourself your own shortcomings or weaknesses take a back seat to the role you are playing.)

On the day of his dress rehearsal, Ralph acts out the part in every detail, and he plays the role to the utmost of his ability. He may fumble his lines or miss a few cues during the dress rehearsal, or maybe for the first few performances, just as an inexperienced actor would. But each day the role becomes more familiar to him and he plays the part more naturally. He follows his script faithfully to the very last detail, the very last letter, each and every day. And he soon reaches a point where he can ad lib here and there and embellish the script to improve the character.

Very soon Ralph begins to feel the motivation of his new character he is portraying. He begins to think and react automatically just as "Bill" thinks and reacts. And then Ralph is no longer merely playing a role. He has acquired a new habit. He has achieved his first short-range goal and is now ready to work towards his second short-range goal by acting the part of "Tom."

Polishing Your Performance

While making a particular movie a professional actor may portray with perfection an outgoing, dynamic character, but perhaps he does not retain these qualities when he is not acting, and off the set he may be shy and retiring. As long as he is acting a part his personal self-consciousness and inhibitions are set aside and forgotten, but he does not continue playing this one role for a long enough period of time to create new attitudes and habits in himself.

However, an actor who plays a continuing role—such as in a television series, a play, or even the same general character in several movies—most often finds himself adopting qualities of the character he is portraying as part of his *own* personality. And he does this without conscious effort or even conscious intent. This is what you will accomplish when you follow your script and act out the part you have written. You will be acting the part of someone else who has a quality you desire—and after a time this quality you wish to acquire will become part of your own personality. And this is only the beginning. You keep writing new scripts and you keep acting the part of someone who possesses each new quality or habit you wish to create in yourself. And after a time you truly become that person you wish so very much to be.

Acting the part may seem awkward to you at first. A new role is awkward to even the most experienced actor until he has polished and perfected his performance. He makes mistakes, he fluffs his lines and he misses cues—at first. But he continues practicing and perfecting his performance until it is faultless. And this is what you do in each new script and each new role, every time you act a part which adds a new dimension to your habits and beliefs.

The "Run" of Your Show

And remember: the professional actor is acting out someone else's script, portraying a character who is the product of someone else's imagination, and his performance continues only for the run of the show. You write your own script, you act the part of a successful person that you really want to be.

Your performance cannot be cancelled until you achieve this new habit, until this acting-image becomes part of the real "you." Your show cannot be closed until you achieve your goal. And then you yourself have closed the show, and you go on to another goal, another script, and another acting-image. When you have reached your goal, when the new habits and new beliefs which were reflected in your acting-image have truly become a part of "you," you go on to another goal and use your acting-image to achieve the new goal. But the habits and beliefs you have developed remain part of your own personality for the rest of your lifetime.

Follow a "Star"

To help you understand a little more about how you can act your part, I would like to use a friend of mine, Macdonald Carey, as an illustration of how a real actor studies his script and learns his lines, and the effort and time he puts into acting his part. Macdonald Carey has enjoyed a long and successful career as an outstanding actor. He is presently playing the starring role in the television series, "Days of Our Lives," on NBC.

Mr. Carey's day begins usually at 5:30 or 6:00 A.M., for he has to be dressed and at the studio by 7:00 A.M., which is the time when everyone assembles on the set. Rehearsals begin promptly, first running through each act two times with no break in the rehearsal. Next comes a run-through of the entire script without benefit of props or scenery, perhaps only a few folding chairs.

The actors now move to the stage on which that day's show is to be filmed, where they then walk through the actions called for in the script for that segment. Then the whole show is put on camera to check proper lighting, camera angles, and the correct positioning of the actors on the set. This is followed by another run-through on camera to coordinate the cameras with the movements of the actors and the action on stage.

At this point a half hour is allotted to criticism aimed towards the polishing and perfecting of the sequence which is about to be filmed. And it is at this time, also, that the actors receive their make-up. This half hour of criticism and make-up is followed by a dress rehearsal, and finally a half-hour break.

After the break there is another period of criticism and any desired changes are made before the program is filmed. Perhaps in the dress rehearsal the timing on a line was not just right, or perhaps someone fluffed a line or two; maybe the set was not exactly right, a chair or some prop was a little bit out of place; possibly one of the actors missed his mark to be properly picked up by the microphone or the camera. Following these last-minute corrections and changes, that day's program is taped. Next, the day's take is viewed and any necessary corrections are made and that portion is reshot. Generally, by this time it is 1:00 in the afternoon. Now, all of this study, all of this rehearsal and work, has been put into the perfecting of one 30-minute program.

And now the actors receive their scripts for the next day's program. Mr. Carey remains at the studio with the other actors, reading, editing, and criticizing the new script until 3:00 or 4:00 p.m., when he finally calls it a day after approximately nine hours of continual concentration, study, criticism, and effort aimed towards the perfecting of his script and his performance in acting a part. And even when he leaves the studio his work is not finished, for he has to study the new script and learn his lines for the following day.

Sounds like an awfully lot of work for one 30-minute segment of filming, doesn't it? But the result is the perfection with which Mr. Carey acts the part he is portraying. He is sincere in his interest and his efforts in his profession. He is meticulous about every detail of every aspect of his work. He became an outstanding actor through good, hard work. He acts his part—that of a doctor, father, and grandfather—with such sincerity and realism that his viewers accept this character as real. Therefore, the program continues to grow and grow in popularity among the viewers, and it becomes more and more successful.

How About You?

Are you willing to put the same amount of interest and time and effort into acting your part as Macdonald Carey does? Your acting-image is vital to your success. You cannot have self–confidence if you do not *act* as if you have self-confidence; you cannot have a magnetic personality if you do not *act* as if you have a magnetic personality; you cannot be successful if you do not *act* successful. You cannot be anything unless you *act* as if you are that something.

If You Do Nothing, You Change Nothing

In this book I have shown you the four major tools, the powers you have within yourself to be a successful individual, regardless of what success means to you. By recognizing and using these tools you can change any habit or belief you wish to change. You can have anything or be anything which is a true, sincere desire on your part.

But notice I said by recognizing and *using* these tools. You can read a different book every day and you can dream and plan and hope. And from your reading you may gain knowledge and an insight into yourself. But if you *do* nothing, you *change* nothing. Even this book, with the unique knowledge and understanding it offers you, will not change you or make you successful simply by the reading alone. You must put these powers and your new knowledge to work for you. You must *use* creative wording, creative imagination, and your acting-image, together with repetition.

Take One Step at a Time

Don't try to change your whole personality all at once. Choose one part which is particularly troublesome to you or the most limiting and make that change your first short-range goal. Write your script with the same meticulous attention to detail and realism as any good script writer does. Then make that script your Bible and follow it faithfully every day until you achieve your goal. Read the script over and over until you understand and know the part you are to play. And then begin to act the part.

Don't be afraid to actually read from the script in the beginning, until you know the part so well you can set your script aside and act the part without it. Concentrate so hard on your script, on acting the part, that your own fears and anxieties and self-consciousness take a back seat to the role you are playing. Remember, you are playing a role, and when you concentrate on acting that part to the best of your ability, your own problems and shortcomings fade to the background.

If you just put a fraction as much effort into acting your part as Macdonald Carey puts into acting his part, you will be able to make any change and achieve any success you want. Through repetition your subconscious will react to the role you are playing. It will accept this experience as real, as a real expression of "you," and it will make this a true part of you and your own habits and beliefs.

And remember, Macdonald Carey is only acting the part of a person someone else has created. You are acting the part of the person you desire to be, the real you, and your "show" is going to run for your entire lifetime. Begin right now to act the part of the person you desire to be—a free, happy, successful individual.

IMPORTANT POINTS TO RECALL

1. Your actions generally conform to what you think about yourself, what you believe about yourself—but these beliefs are frequently false.
2. Your habits and beliefs were acquired from past conditioning, and can be changed by reconditioning.
3. Acting-image is another major tool or power for creating success.
4. Acting-image is extremely effective because it combines the powers of creative wording, creative imagination and

repetition, and adds a new dimension of acting the part.

5. You have used this tool many times in the past without being aware of it, for example, when you learned to walk, type, drive a car, etc. A major portion of your physical actions and gestures, your personality, has been created through an acting-image.

6. To make the best use of this tool, write out a script depicting a character who has the habits, beliefs or abilities you wish to acquire.

7. Your script must be written in vivid detail and must show your "star" as possessing these qualities here and now.

8. When you repeatedly act the part of the person you want to become or act the part of a person who possesses a habit or belief or quality you wish to acquire, your subconscious reacts to this experiencing and is conditioned to react automatically. This new habit or quality becomes a part of "you."

9. Once your script is prepared, you must follow it faithfully and act the part every day.

10. You cannot discard that particular acting-image until you have achieved your goal. Then you go on to another goal, another script, and another acting-image.

11. These tools will not create anything or achieve your goals for you unless you actually *use* the tools.

CHAPTER NINE

Creating Actual
Success Habits

Setting your goals is an extremely important part of your progress. Figure 4 is a drawing of a tower which consists of a stairway leading to the top, with landings at various points along the way, and windows through which you can look to gauge your progress in ascending the tower.

Obviously, if you were to climb the tower you would have to start at the bottom, at the first step of the stairway in order to reach the top.

Stairway to Success

And in a sense this is what you are doing now. You are climbing your own personal stairway. And your goal is perfection in every phase of your life.

You have already climbed several stairs:

- 1st Step: You climbed the first step of your stairway when you gained an understanding of the real "you," when you learned about your conscious mind and your subconscious, their relationship to each other, and the duties and responsibilities of each.

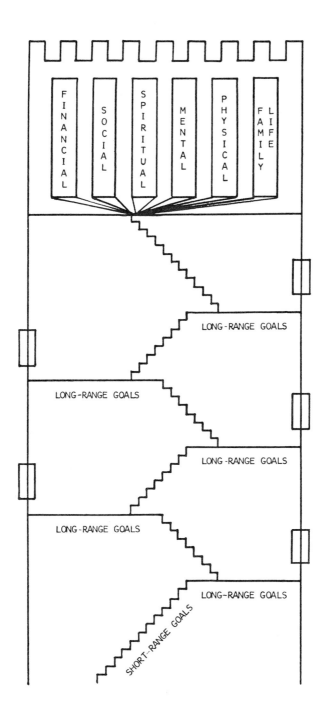

Figure 4

- 2nd Step: You achieved the second step of your stairway by learning the basic tools and influences which conditioned you in the past and molded and forged the present "you." You now know the origin of your present beliefs and attitudes.
- 3rd Step: The third step was attained when you discovered the power of creative wording, and when you learned how it has influenced you in the past and how you can use it to create your future successes.
- 4th Step: You reached the fourth step when you became aware of the tremendous power you have through your creative imagination and the part it has played in your past conditioning and the part it can play in achieving your goals and desires for the future.
- 5th Step: The fifth step was mounted when you developed the art of relaxation-concentration and began to remove fear and tension from your life.
- 6th Step: You conquered the sixth step when you learned how to open the lines of communication between your conscious mind and your subconscious. This will enable you to communicate more directly with the subconscious and use the tools more effectively to gain the most rapid and complete mastery of your subconscious and your future.
- 7th Step: You took the very important seventh step when you recognized the existence and power of a Universal Force with which you can communicate and from which you can receive guidance and answers without conscious effort.
- 8th Step: And you climbed the eighth step of your stairway when you learned to condition your subconscious to make any change you desire through your acting-image by acting the part of the person you sincerely desire to be.

Where Are You Now?

You are now at the first landing of your new stairway to

success, and you can rest for just a moment before you continue on. While you are resting, look out the window of this landing and enjoy the pleasant view. The view you see from this landing is indeed very pleasant because it is comprised in part of all the knowledge you gained as you climbed those first eight stairs. From this landing you have a new understanding of yourself: who and what you are, and *why* you are that person.

Another part of the view is the knowledge that you have right within you every tool, every talent, every power to be exactly the person you want to be and to achieve every success you ever desired, even far beyond those successes you have dreamed of in the past.

You have with you on this first landing the knowledge, tools, and power to build the remainder of your stairway to your successes in life. All you have to do is use this knowledge and these tools and continue building up and up and up. There is absolutely nothing that can limit the height to which you can build unless you yourself impose some limitation.

Stairs and Landings

From this first landing, each short-range goal which you accomplish becomes another step in your stairway. And each long-range goal you achieve becomes another landing, each one higher than the previous ones.

And the view from each successive landing becomes more and more beautiful because it consists of all the goals and successes you have achieved along the way.

There Are No Stopping Places

These landings are never stopping points, merely resting places where you can feel the accomplishments you have achieved. And at each landing you gain greater faith in yourself and renewed energies for the next long-range goal.

Your Stairway Is One-Way Only

Your stairway is unique in many ways, but one facet of its uniqueness is that it's one-way only. You never turn around and go down the stairs; you are always climbing higher and higher.

You never rest long enough at any landing to say, "I am a success." Each step and each landing marks another successful accomplishment, and you rest only long enough to think, "I am successful; and I continue to be more successful in the future with every step I take." You continue to achieve goal after goal, step after step. Always progressing, and never going backwards.

A Guide in Formulating Goals

Sometimes it is difficult to know exactly what you want, and without planned goals you cannot achieve anything. You, yourself, of course, must pick your own goals. But I would like to discuss, very briefly, the six major areas of life and give you a guide which I believe will help you in formulating your goals.

Ultimate Goals

I'm sure the terms "long-range goal" and "short-range goal" are very familiar to you. There is, however, a third type of goal which you should establish and work towards, and that is an *ultimate* goal. You should have an ultimate goal which you are always working towards in each of the six major areas of life.

At the top of the stairway in your tower, visualize a beautiful room representing these six basic areas. Each step of your stairway takes you closer; and you are always climbing upwards towards this beautiful room—your ultimate goal—at the top of your tower.

Once you have definitely established your ultimate goal, then you need give it no great amount of thought or concern. Simply keep it in the back of your mind as the ultimate destination towards which you progress through each and every short-range goal and long-range goal you achieve.

Perfection—Your Ultimate Goal

Your ultimate goal should be perfection in every area of life. When I say "ultimate" and "perfection" I realize that these are very final and absolute conditions; but I mean the words literally. The frequently used phrase, "Nobody is perfect," may certainly be true; and perhaps your first reaction to my use of the word "perfection" is that no one but an egotist or a radical would even expect perfection from a human being. Well, while it may certainly be true that "Nobody is perfect," it is equally true that no one that we know of has ever used more than a minor portion of his talents and powers *in an effort to be perfect.*

We are told, "Be ye perfect even as thy Father in heaven is perfect." Surely we would not be exhorted to be perfect if that was an impossibility, a meaningless exercise in futility. We each have within us every requirement and every power to be perfect. In the past we simply had not progressed enough to know how to use these powers to that extent. If we do not establish perfection as our ultimate goal, we will never progress to the point where human beings can be perfect. If we aspire to anything less than perfection, we have implied doubt in these powers we have and we have placed a limitation on ourselves.

I don't wish to belabor this point, but it is such an important one and I feel so very strongly about it, that I will dwell on it a moment longer. It is a sad commentary on human beings—or "human nature" as we are prone to phrase it in apologizing for lack of strength or integrity—that we find it more and more convenient to accept mediocrity and increasingly difficult to envision perfection, let alone to strive for it ourselves. If we would make a sincere effort to be perfect, if we would set perfection as our ultimate goal, then mankind could experience a halt in its retreat from perfection or even a turning point towards perfection which would make its attainment possible.

So I repeat: Your ultimate goal should be absolute perfection in every area of life. Any lesser goal constitutes a limitation which you are placing upon yourself. And the removal of all limitations is the largest single step you can take towards a successful future.

A Financial Goal

Since money is vitally important to most people, let's discuss the financial area of life first. What goal could possibly be construed to be perfection in this area? A million dollars? Ten million dollars? A billion dollars? Would that be perfection as far as you are concerned?

Let's say you have devised a plan to earn a certain sum of money. Now, what does this money mean to you? What would this money do for you? What would you do with the money? Would you put it in the bank for future use or would you invest it for the future? And if so, why?

When you save money or put it in the bank or invest it, you do so because you want to know the money is always there in case you want to spend it for something or have a need for it, don't you? You want the money available so when you do want it or need it, it's there.

Would it be perfection to you if you had enough money for a beautiful home and clothes, nice automobiles; money enough, really, to buy anything or do anything you want? If you have money in the bank, the only time you take the money out is when you want to buy something or spend it, isn't that correct? You don't carry the money around with you in your pocket; you just want to know it's available to you whenever you want to spend some of it. Therefore, you might state your ultimate financial goal as: "I always have enough money to use as I desire."

Let's assume you have a million dollars in cash. You might keep it in a vault at home, but you wouldn't carry it around with you, I'm sure. Let's pretend also that you are the master of a magic genie, and every time you want to buy something, whether it's a hamburger, a necktie, a new house, a yacht, or anything else you desire, all you have to do is speak or think of the amount you want and your little genie immediately appears and hands you the money, regardless of how little or how much you want.

With your magic genie serving you, it would be rather unimportant whether you had that million dollars or not, wouldn't it? I'm sure you would never carry it with you; you probably wouldn't ever take it out of the vault because there would be no need to.

So you see, in effect you only want enough money to pay for whatever you want whenever you want it. And this ultimate goal would be correct: "I always have enough money to use as I desire."

A Spiritual Goal

What is your idea of perfection in the spiritual area of your life? What would be your ultimate goal? To attend church more regularly? To donate more to your church? To become a better person? But each of these goals is very narrow—and each of them is limited. What, then, would be considered perfection in the spiritual area?

In the Bible we are told, "The disciple is not above his master, but everyone that is perfect shall be as his master." And also, "The Father and I are one, the same as the Father and you are one," and we are admonished to "...be one with the Father."

This certainly would be perfection, wouldn't it: to be one with the Father? It would be an ultimate, unlimited goal. And anyone who adopted such an ultimate goal as his sincere desire would become an infinitely better person. So as an ultimate goal in the spiritual area of your life you could state: "I am one with the Father."

A Family Life Goal

There are many goals you could choose to work towards to improve this particular area of your life: more love and affection from your mate; better communication and better understanding between you and your children or spouse or other members of the family; more time to spend with your family, more good times together as a family unit; no bickering or arguing among members of the family.

All of these goals are good and you would receive benefit from each and every one of them. But again they are limited and cover only narrow portions of overall family life. When you analyze all of these goals, the one thing you truly desire is absolute family harmony. This is unlimited and it covers the full spectrum of family life. Therefore, as your ultimate goal in the area of your family life, you could say, "I have absolute family harmony."

A Social Goal

A discussion of the social area of your life could go on and on indefinitely. And you could recite goal after goal to improve your social life. You want people to like you and accept you. You want people to enjoy your company. You want to meet more people and be more socially active. You want to meet people who have similar interests.

As I said, you could name countless goals in the social area of your life. But again in analyzing all these goals, each one covers only one small aspect of social life. And each goal is limited. But all of these goals would have an ultimate purpose in common because human beings have one common desire in this area. Everyone wants to be loved and accepted and respected by other people. Nobody wants to be alone. And the one answer to each of these goals and the one answer that fulfills this common desire is "true friends."

True friends do love you and accept you and respect you. They enjoy your company and you enjoy theirs. They have, or develop, similar interests because they are your friends. And with many true friends you certainly become more socially active and meet even more people. You are not alone or lonely.

So as an unlimited goal, an ultimate goal which would bring

perfection in your social life, you can say: "I have many true friends."

A Mental Goal

In the mental area of your life, I believe the ultimate goal is more obvious. We all desire to be "smart," to have great knowledge and intelligence. I am sure everyone, if it were possible for him, would desire to be a mental genius, to know everything.

You now know that you do have access to a Universal Force which has Universal Knowledge. And you know that once you learn to communicate with this Universal Force you can draw upon this knowledge and power and create anything you may desire, provided your desire is good and right. It is only natural that we all want to have this Universal Knowledge.

In truth you already have access to this knowledge; but perhaps you have not yet learned absolute faith and do not "feel" within you the truthfulness of this fact. Therefore, as an ultimate goal to attain perfection in this mental area of life, you may say: "I have Universal Knowledge."

A Physical Goal

Our consideration of the physical area of your life is limited to only your physical body. And there may be many things related to your body which you would desire to improve or change.

Perhaps you desire to be physically able to perform particular activities or participate in certain sports. Possibly you desire to have more strength, more stamina, vitality and energy. Maybe you simply wish to eliminate a headache or a head cold. What you are really desirous of, ultimately, is perfect health.

Possibly even perfect health isn't quite enough. You might still not be satisfied with your physical appearance because you feel you are underweight or overweight or there is some certain thing about your physical body which does not please you.

What you really want is to have a perfect body. Therefore, as your ultimate unlimited goal to achieve perfection in the physical area you could say: "My body is absolute perfection."

Your Ultimate Goal Includes:

Financial—"I *always* have *enough money* to use as I desire."
Spiritual—"I am *one with the Father.*"
Family Life—"I have *absolute* family *harmony.*"
Social—"I have *many true friends.*"
Mental—"I have *universal knowledge.*"
Physical—"My *body* is absolute *perfection.*"

Remove All Limitations

Each of these goals expresses perfection in the specific area in which it is related. None of them is limited in any way.

I fully realize that you have been conditioned in the past to place limitations on your thinking and on your goals, but you must remove these limitations you have placed on yourself. Every limitation you remove is a giant step in your stairway to success.

Because we have been conditioned to place limitations on our thinking and on our goals, it is frequently difficult for people to accept ideas or things which are new to them. But even if you are such a person and you are finding it difficult to have absolute faith in your potential attainment of these ultimate goals I have suggested, I would ask you to keep an open mind about them. Having such goals certainly cannot harm you or hurt you in any way. Adopting them as your ultimate goals for your life is another step towards your successful future.

Napoleon Hill stated in his book *Think and Grow Rich* (Hawthorne Books, Inc.), "There are no limitations to the mind except what we acknowledge." And I say to you now that there is absolutely nothing you can't do, nothing you can't have, if you believe you can achieve it.

I have given you the HOW. I have shown you the power you have within you. I have told you of the tools you have available to you. I have explained to you how they work and some of the reasons why they work. All you have to do now is put them to use.

Select Your First Goal

Let's begin to put your new knowledge and these tools to work towards your successful future now. It's time to select your first long-range goal which you are going to achieve.

I'm sure there are many things you want in life. And when you begin to write these down (as you will shortly) you will think of even dozens more that may escape your attention right at this moment. But how do you pick that very first, all-important long-range goal to work towards?

Desire Is the Beginning

The first thing you must have before selecting or defining your goal is "desire." Desire is the beginning, the starting point for each and every achievement.

And before you have an opportunity to think or say, "I know what I want. I know what my desire is. But can I get it?" let me repeat again: There is no limitation to what you can achieve if your desire is strong enough and if you use the tools you have right within you.

Emerson expressed this important truth beautifully when he said, "There is nothing capricious in nature and the implanting of a desire indicates that its gratification is in the constitution of the creature that feels it." In other words, there is nothing that you are capable of wanting or desiring that you are not capable of achieving. If you did not have within you the ability to fulfill a desire, you would not feel that desire in the first place.

Proper Motivation

When you feel a sincere desire, you feel motivated to take action to gratify that desire, to achieve it. Now, when I speak of motivation, I mean personal motivation that comes from within you, not outside motivations. I mean motivation within yourself that springs from a sincere desire and your belief in your ability to accomplish that goal.

Formulate Your Desires into Words

Take time now to think about your desires. What changes do you want to make in yourself in order to become the person you sincerely want to be? What do you desire to do or to be? What type of future do you want?

It is very important that you write these desires down, that you actually put these desires into words on paper. Carry a small notebook with you for the next few days. Every time you think of some desire you have, some goal you would like to achieve, write it down in the book.

Don't be concerned with categorizing your goals at this point. Simply write each one down as it comes to mind. As you begin achieving your goals, one after the other, and as you progress and become more successful, you will continually acquire new goals and new desires, and some of the goals you are writing down right now may change or be eliminated.

Your First Long-Range Goal

After you have compiled a list of your current desires, study your list and choose one goal and make this your first long-range goal to work towards.

It is preferred that for your first few long-range goals you select goals which will help you, as an individual, to develop and improve yourself rather than something of a monetary or material nature. Later, when you have more experience in the proper use of these tools and you thoroughly understand the true power you have, then you can choose anything you desire as a goal. But the most important thing to accomplish in the beginning is to develop yourself.

Work on One Goal at a Time

Please notice that I emphasized that you select only one goal. This does not mean that the other goals will be forgotten or discarded; but you can work towards only one long-range goal at a time, and all other goals temporarily take a back seat to the one you are working towards at a given time.

Each goal you work towards will be more easily accomplished than the ones preceding it. But no matter how rapidly you progress, no matter with what speed you are able to achieve each goal, you continue to work towards only one long-range goal at a time.

Steps Between Landings

Remember that each long-range goal becomes a landing on the stairway in your tower. And between each landing you must have several small steps you take to reach the landing. These smaller steps are the short-range goals you achieve to fulfill your long-range goal.

So carefully analyze your first goal you have chosen and then break it down into several steps, each of which takes you one step closer to your long-range goal. You can break this down into as many steps as you wish, but it is preferable to have somewhere between five and ten steps to achieve a long-range goal, depending, of course, on how big your long-range goal is.

A Natural Progression of Steps

In breaking any long-range goal down into short-range goals, there is a natural progression of accomplishments or steps. One accomplishment must be made before the second one can be approached. Then the second step must be accomplished before you can approach the third step. When you break down your long-range goals you should see this natural progression of steps and put them in their proper sequence or proper order.

You Can't Stop in the Middle of a Step

You may change any goal, whether it be a short-range goal or a long-range goal, at any time you wish, EXCEPT THE ONE SHORT-RANGE GOAL YOU ARE WORKING ON AT THE IMMEDIATE TIME.

This is something I cannot stress too strongly. You can never change or discard the one short-range goal you are working on at any particular time. Remember, you are conditioning your subconscious. You are learning to master your subconscious. And you are creating new habits of successful achievements. If you change the one short-range goal you are working on or terminate that goal before you achieve it, you are conditioning your subconscious to a habit of failure. You are "crying wolf" to your subconscious, and you are conditioning him to quit in the middle of all your goals—and success will never be yours.

So please bear in mind at all times that you cannot quit in the middle of the short-range goal you are working on. You must fulfill that step you have communicated to your subconscious as your sincere desire. You must accomplish that particular goal, or you are conditioning your subconscious not to react to your desires, and you are creating a habit of failure.

You can change or eliminate any future goals, either short-range or long-range, but *never the step or short-range goal you are working on at the immediate time.*

Short-Range Goals

Let's go back for a few minutes to Ralph who wanted to become a successful salesman. This was his long-range goal.

Ralph knew that the first change he had to make in his own habits before he could be successful in any endeavor was to overcome his tendency to lie in bed in the mornings and to start each day physically sluggish and mentally at low ebb. So his first short-range goal was to form a habit of arising immediately when the alarm went off, exercising for 15 minutes, and taking a brisk shower—just as Bill does. Ralph began to act the part of

"Bill," in this one respect only, until his subconscious reacted to this experiencing and made this morning routine a natural habit.

Ralph knew that no matter how qualified he was, no matter what his abilities were, he could not be really successful unless he made an impression on people which was favorable enough that they would afford him the time to listen to his sales presentation. Therefore, his second short-range goal was to look like a successful salesman. Once his first short-range goal was achieved and he had acquired a new habit which enables him to begin each day mentally and physically alert, then he began to act the part of those attributes he had observed in Tom. He acted the part of "Tom" who was immaculately groomed, dressed in clean, neat clothing that was suitable for his profession, and looked every bit the part of the successful business man. And again Ralph acted this part until he had formed a new habit and made this quality a natural part of his true self. He had then formed two new habits which contributed greatly to his future successes and he had achieved his first two short-range goals.

Ralph continued on this way, acting the part of the different people who possessed qualities which Ralph wished to create in himself. But he worked on only one step, playing one role at a time, until he created a new habit which became a natural part of Ralph's true self.

A Change of Mind

Ralph wanted to become a very successful salesman and was working towards that long-range goal. Up to now he never really thought he could be anything else. However, after achieving a few short-range goals, Ralph gained the attitude that he could have what he wanted and could be anything he truly wanted to be. He had long had an interest in becoming a doctor, but his belief in himself had always been that he was incapable of the study and the self-discipline required. By the time he achieved a few short-range goals, he had proven to himself that he was capable of learning anything he had a desire to learn. He had acquired new habits and new beliefs about himself. He discarded his long-range goal of becoming a successful salesman and established a new long-range goal: to become a doctor.

What About Obstacles?

You have now chosen your first long-range goal. You have broken it down into several steps, or short-range goals. And you have begun to work towards accomplishing that very first short-range goal.

It would be ridiculous to assume that obstacles will never arise; but no obstacles can keep you from attaining your goals unless you let them. This is one reason why you must have a planned, sincere desire to accomplish something before you can really achieve it. Only a planned, sincere desire will generate within you the motivation to fulfill that desire and overcome any and all obstacles along the way.

Let's take a closer look at what the real obstacles might be. You know that these very tools you are now using to create a new and successful future can, and often do, work against you as well as for you. The only real obstacles in your path toward this successful life are those which have been created by these very tools which have worked against you in the past, and which may still be working against you at the present time. In earlier chapters you have recognized many of these obstacles and learned how to overcome them.

Removing Stumbling Blocks

You, as a free individual, as the master of your subconscious, must locate these obstacles and remove them. Examine your present habits, the words you use, your thoughts, the pictures you create in your imagination, and find out what you are presently doing that could become an obstacle in the path of completing your goal.

Ask yourself questions such as: "What habits do I now have that might keep me from accomplishing my goal? What mental pictures do I find myself with that could stop me? What words do I repeat over and over daily that could hold me back?" Examine yourself carefully and critically. When you find that you have a habit that would impede your progress towards a particular goal, use these very same tools—creative wording, creative imagination, acting-image and repetition—to remove that habit and replace it with a new and useful one.

If you find yourself with a thought that you may not be able to achieve your goal, immediately replace it with the thought that you already have it, it is yours. And use your creative imagination to create a mental picture of your goal, picturing it as already being accomplished, already being yours or a part of you. In the next chapter you will learn a method of using key words and key letters to actually control your thinking and negate any detrimental thoughts.

If you catch yourself using harmful creative wording such as "I don't understand. I don't know how. I don't remember. I can't get going. I haven't enough time. Something is wrong with me. I don't believe," eliminate these expressions. Replace them with creative wording which motivates your subconscious to react and materialize your goal instead of giving him these harmful suggestions with your own thoughtless remarks.

For instance, if you catch yourself using the expression, "I don't understand," immediately cancel that suggestion out by stating, "That's nonsense. I understand very clearly." If you should say, "I don't know how," cancel the suggestion at once with the suggestion, "That's not correct. I certainly know how." If you should say, "I don't remember," that is foolish. Replace it with the statement, "I recall everything as I need it." The comment, "I can't get going," should be replaced at once with the suggestion, "Of course I can get going. I have an abundance of energy." If you have the thought or make the statement, "I haven't enough time," cancel such a harmful suggestion immediately with the suggestion, "I have all the time I need."

Keep Your Goals a Private Matter

Keep your desires and your goals private, a secret between you and your subconscious. Your desires create mental pictures or impressions in your mind; and this is a form of energy. When you show people or tell other people your plans, you dispel this energy, thereby delaying the fulfillment of your goals or failing completely. This energy should be applied towards achieving your goals rather than being expended in discussing them.

Do not make a tremendous effort to keep your goals a secret. Simply refrain from discussing them with other people. Not only do you dispel this energy when you talk about your goals, but you also subject yourself to the negative thoughts and words of others. Those people who have no knowledge of the power within themselves, who are failure-prone because of the many limitations they have imposed on themselves, are generally anxious to justify their own lack of faith and their own limitations by imposing them on others. And they do this through skepticism, criticism, and often even ridicule.

Again, if you believe in yourself and the power you possess as a free, creative being, and if you are the true master of your subconscious, you can use your judgment in evaluating these negative suggestions and discard them completely and not pass them on to your subconscious. But it certainly serves no purpose to open yourself to such influences in the first place. So keep your business—your desires and goals—to yourself.

Anything Is Possible

In the next chapter some additional aids are explained which you can use in achieving your goals. You must understand, however, that there is no struggle or strain or real effort required for you to accomplish your goals. Just carry the correct thought; use the correct words—out loud; act the part; and use repetition; and you are well on your way to getting what you really desire.

You can accomplish goal after goal, one at a time, and you

can create any future successes you wish to have. Remember, there is nothing you are capable of wanting or desiring that you are not capable of achieving.

IMPORTANT POINTS TO RECALL

1. True success includes every phase of life: spiritual, social, physical, financial, mental, and family life.
2. Setting your goals is an extremely important part of your progress.
3. You have taken several giant strides towards success in the knowledge you have gained from this book.
4. You should set three types of goals: ultimate, long-range, and short-range goals.
5. You should always be working towards your ultimate goal covering each of the six major areas of life, and this ultimate goal should represent perfection in each of the six areas.
6. Any goal less than perfection is a limitation which you are placing upon yourself.
7. Desire is the beginning or starting point for each goal and each achievement.
8. There is nothing which you are capable of desiring which you are not also capable of achieving.
9. You should write down all your desires, and then select one as your first long-range goal.
10. Long-range goals should be broken down into between five and ten short-range goals, depending on how big the long-range goal is.
11. Short-range goals should follow a natural progression towards achievement of the long-range goal.
12. You can work on only one short-range goal at a time.
13. You may change or discard any future goal, either long- or short-range. But you can *never change the immediate short-range goal you are working on* at any particular time.
14. Keep your goals private, a secret between you and your subconscious.

CHAPTER TEN

Special Aids and How to Use Them

I am sure that in the past you have set many goals for yourself. But it is most probable that these goals were neither properly selected nor properly pursued.

In the past you have tried to fulfill your desires and needs by conscious effort and willpower. You have tried through sheer determination to break habits and to change certain aspects of your personality which were objectionable to yourself or to others. And you have tried to form new, successful habits and beliefs in yourself by again applying willpower and self-determination. Many times your efforts to accomplish these goals failed because the goals themselves were not properly established. And even more often your efforts to achieve these goals were thwarted because you did not know how to use the tools and powers which you have within you.

You have now learned the proper method of establishing three types of goals. Because you now realize you are absolutely unlimited in your power and ability to achieve anything you desire, you have established ultimate goals which represent perfection in each of the six basic areas of life. You have carefully considered your present desires and have compiled a list of goals from which you have selected one as your first long-range goal to work towards. With your new understanding of how each long-range goal is broken down into short-range goals which follow a natural progression towards the accomplishment of the long-range goal, you have chosen your very first short-range goal and are ready to begin working towards its fulfillment.

The Easy Way and the Only Way

To accomplish this first short-range goal—or any future goal—you do not use great willpower and conscious effort as you did in the past. You do not struggle and fret and feel the frustration you have often felt in the past. And you will not fail as you have sometimes done in the past.

You have learned of the four basic tools and the tremendous power you possess when you use them properly. No matter what your goal may be, you can always use these tools—creative wording, creative imagination, acting-image, and repetition—to achieve any goal successfully without effort or struggle.

Now that you are aware at last of the existence of these tools and this tremendous power within you, and now that you understand how to use them properly to create what you want instead of letting them operate without your guidance and work against you, you will find it very simple, very easy to apply them in creating a future full of happiness and contentment and successes beyond any that you dared to dream of in the past.

Many Aids Are Available

In addition to the ease with which you can create with these tools and the power they generate, you have aids available to you in implementing the tools and hastening their effectiveness.

We have already liscussed some of these aids: relaxation-concentration; "sleeping on it"; self-hypnosis; the pendulum; and automatic writing. These are all aids in establishing better communications through which you can convey your desires to your subconscious and the Universal Force.

A Visual Aid

I would now like to expand on one powerful aid in achieving your goals. I have no way of knowing, of course, what your personal goals are; but whatever they might be, this aid is extremely valuable to you in accomplishing them.

On a blank sheet of paper create an actual detailed picture of your immediate *short-range* goal. This is very simple to do. Create a mental image of your goal and then compose that picture on the sheet of paper. You can compose your picture from cut-outs from magazines or catalogs. You can use photographs. If you have an artistic bent, you can draw or paint the picture.

Here and Now

Remember, you are the one who is composing this picture and you are creating a picture of what you want. Always bear in mind that when you use creative wording you express your goal as existing here and now; when you use your creative imagination, you imagine your goal as already yours here and now; when you create an acting-image you act the part as here and now. This picture you are composing must also show your goal as here and now. And it must be in vivid detail.

Composing a Picture

For example, suppose you desire to own a new Continental and you establish that as your immediate goal. You can cut out a picture of this car from a magazine or brochure and paste it on your sheet of paper. You can cut out a picture of yourself from a photograph and place it in the car to "put yourself in the picture" and show that the car is yours, you already have it.

Make sure, though, if at all possible, that the picture you use is the exact make, model, color, etc., of the car you want. If your picture shows a 4-door model when you really want the 2-door, you may very well wind up with the 4-door model. If you want a canary yellow car but use a picture of one that is fire-engine red, don't be surprised if your new Continental is fire-engine red.

So create a picture depicting your goal in as vivid detail—and as exact detail—as you possibly can. In the case of the Continental you could take a picture of your home and impose the picture of the Continental on it as though the car were sitting in front of your house. If you are particularly enterprising, you might even go so far as to have a car salesman bring out the exact model and color Continental you desire and have him park it in your driveway while you take a picture. Or have the salesman take a picture of you sitting in the car in front of your home.

When your picture is completed showing your goal in vivid detail as already being yours, it is yours here and now, you have created a very powerful visual aid.

A Visual Aid in Losing Weight

Let me give you an illustration of just how powerful visual aids really are. I once had as a client a young lady who was 21 years old and weighed *297 pounds*. This young woman came from a family of considerable means and she had been exposed to an endless flow of diets and treatments and various methods and controls to get her to lose weight. She had seen several specialists. But she did not respond to any of the attempts to induce her to lose this very unsightly excess weight.

There is no purpose to be served at this time in explaining to you the reason for this girl's weight problem or her attitude towards life in general at that particular time. It is sufficient you know that because of circumstances which had occurred during this period in her life she was extremely rebellious towards her family, her religion, her schooling, and life in general. Her weight problem was an expression of that rebellion and she *did not want to lose weight.* She came under my care only through the insistence of her parents.

Because of her rebellious attitude and her complete lack of desire to improve herself or make any change in her appearance, this girl did not respond to any type of treatment. She had such a low degree of susceptibility to hypnosis that it was not effective in working with her. Because she did not want to lose weight, when her physician prescribed a diet, she would not follow it. If exercises were prescribed, she would not exercise. She rebelled against anything and everything she thought might possibly be successful in causing her to lose weight, and she would not follow through on any advice or suggestions given.

She only continued to come to me for counselling because of her father's insistence. Up to that point we had made no progress towards reducing the weight problem. But we had made some small strides in changing her attitude and conduct at home. Because of this improvement, her father refused to let her quit because at least at home they could live with her, and he held some hope for further improvement.

After working with this young woman for a considerable period of time I finally arrived at a method to get her to react. I knew all too well from past experience with her that if she thought a procedure would work at all, she would not follow through with it. However, if she was firmly convinced that a particular plan would not work, she would cooperate out of contrariness and as a means of pacifying her parents.

I told this girl to have many pictures taken of her own face. Then she was to take pictures of slender, shapely models from magazines and catalogs and to cut out the pictures of her own face from the photographs and impose them on the models in the pictures. She was instructed to place these pictures around her room, in her car, around the swimming pool, beside the mirrors she used—anywhere she would see them. And every time she looked at one of these pictures she was to say, "There I am. That's what I look like. That's me."

She complied with this procedure because it was something tangible she could do which would mollify her parents—and because she felt sure there would be no results forthcoming from it. I am sure if she had really known just how effective the suggestions from the pictures, these visual aids, were going to be when combined with the creative wording I instructed her to use, and if she had known what results would be created, she would have rebelled at this plan just as she had rebelled at all the others. But she did as she was told and used the pictures and the creative wording because she doubted the results. However, even her doubts in the results could not prevent the results from occurring when she used the visual aids and the creative wording as she was instructed.

To insure there would be no results, she began buying 2-pound boxes of candy which she would eat every day while lounging around the swimming pool at her home. And she kept me informed of the amount of candy she was buying and consuming so I would be aware that I was putting nothing over on her and that my plan would not work.

For the next ten months, nothing happened; and she was very happy in her own rebellious way. But at the end of ten months she began losing weight. The first few weeks she lost about a pound a week—very slight. Then a few weeks more and she started losing about a pound and a half a week. Then two pounds a week. Then two and a half. She finally reached the point where she was losing three to three and a half pounds a week on a regular basis.

She began buying 5-pound boxes of candy, and then even 10-pound boxes. She sat around the swimming pool in the sun eating the candy and trying to put the weight back on—and she couldn't stop the weight loss. She "ate like a horse"—and she still couldn't stop it. She said, "I eat everything, but I can't stop losing weight."

Today this young woman weighs 127 pounds. She actually looks like those models in the pictures she used. After such a tremendous weight loss it took almost another year to tighten the loose skin, but by that time she was willing to do whatever was necessary because she could see how very attractive she could be.

As her appearance improved, her disposition and her

personality improved also. Young men suddenly became very attentive and she began having dates and living a happy, healthy, normal life for a young woman.

Create an Exact Mental Picture

So visual aids do work. Why? Because they help you create an exact mental picture in your mind. Keep this in mind, and compose your picture with care. Whether you create your own picture by drawing it, using cut-outs from magazines, catalogs, brochures, etc., take photographs, or compose a picture using all these sources, be sure to create a picture (or many pictures) showing your own goal in absolute, vivid detail as already yours now.

Use Key Words and Key Letters

And now we come to another aid which reinforces the effectiveness of each of the four major tools. This is an aid which also, in a sense, enables you to actually control your own thinking by means of assigning a key letter or a key word to your goal.

Write Down Your Suggestion

On a second blank sheet of paper, prepare a creatively worded suggestion for your goal. This is also very easy to do. Let's continue to assume that your immediate goal is to own a new Continental but your present finances do not permit you to buy it. You have already composed your picture, your visual aid, which shows you sitting in the driver's seat of the car, or the car sitting in front of your house, or indicating in some way that the car belongs to you, it is yours. With this picture in mind, you would write your worded suggestion such as, "This Continental is mine. I own it. I already have it."

Include All Necessary Restrictions

Now, anybody can go down and buy a new car if they can squeeze the downpayment out of the budget. But this is not your intention, so you want to place certain conditions upon your ownership of this beautiful new car. Therefore, you continue with your worded suggestion by stating: "I own it. I do not owe anything on it. It is mine free and clear." In other words, if you were to state your worded suggestion, "This Continental is mine," period, with no conditions or restrictions, if your credit was good you could go down and buy the Continental. Then the car would be yours, but you would owe a tremendous amount of money on it.

So your suggestion must be stated in a creative manner, saying that you already have it, it is already yours, and include the restrictions that you owe nothing on it, the insurance and license are paid for, the Continental is yours, free and clear, and you have no encumbrances whatever in regards to the car.

Include All Necessary Exclusions

There are also certain exclusions which you should place on every goal concerning the manner in which it will be attained. One of the major problems in the world today is that people try to achieve their personal desires through any available means without regard for the consequences to themselves or others. I'm sure you probably know of men and women who strive for financial or professional success through any avenues open to them and who lose their families, their friends, or the respect of their associates as a result. This is particularly tragic because every worthwhile goal can be reached without harm to yourself or others.

As an illustration, let's say you want this new Continental very badly and you are determined to have it and you don't care how you get it. With this attitude, some member of your family whom you dearly love might be involved in an accident where he is not at fault but in which he receives serious injuries which would disable him or practically destroy his life. Because this member of your family was not at fault in the accident, the insurance company representing the driver of the other car would make a substantial financial settlement with you covering damages. You now have the money to go down and pay cash for the Continental. It is yours free and clear, with no encumbrances—but at what price to yourself and others in grief and pain.

Exclusions Will Not Hinder or Delay You

You can have the new car just as quickly with exclusions as to how your goal is to be achieved as without them. These exclusions in no way interfere in your attaining your goal.

So included in your written suggestion would be a statement such as: "I received this Continental without harm or suffering or loss of any kind to myself or any other person."

Assign a Symbol to Your Goal

After you have composed your picture as a visual aid, and after you have prepared your creatively worded suggestion that your goal is yours, the conditions under which it is yours, and the exclusion of harm to yourself or anyone else in achieving it, then you sum up *both* your picture and your worded suggestion in a KEY WORD or KEY LETTER which becomes a symbol for your goal until you achieve it.

It's entirely up to you what you use for a key word or a key letter. But bear in mind that your subconscious cannot reason and therefore it reacts literally to this key word or letter. Also, it is always more advantageous to use a word that is descriptive of your goal. Assuming again that the Continental is your goal, you might use the letter "C" or the word "Continental" as the symbol for your goal.

Use This Summarization

When you have chosen the key word or letter you wish to use to sum up and symbolize your immediate goal, then on the second sheet of paper immediately after your worded suggestion which contains the restrictions and exclusions pertaining to the goal, write the following summarization: "All of this suggestion and all of this picture are summed up in the letter 'C'. The letter 'C' is my symbol for this goal. Every time I speak the letter 'C', every time I think the letter 'C', every time I hear the letter 'C', and every time I see the letter 'C', my goal dominates my thoughts and becomes stronger every time. All of this picture and all of this suggestion are summed up in the letter 'C'."

This summarization for your key word or key letter is to be written on the same sheet of paper immediately following your written suggestion. Obviously, you would insert the key letter or key word you yourself have selected. And if you have composed several pictures rather than just one you would change the paragraph to read, "All of *these pictures* . . ." But otherwise the summarization must be written with the exact wording I have given you. This is extremely important for the effectiveness of these key words and key letters, so let me repeat this wording for you again, assuming that you have now chosen the letter "X" as your key letter:

> "All of this suggestion and all of this picture are summed up in the letter X. The letter X is my symbol for this goal. Every time I speak the letter X, every time I think the letter X, every time I hear the letter X, and every time I see the letter X, my goal dominates my thoughts and becomes stronger every time. All of this picture and all of this suggestion are summed up in the letter X."

Reinforce Your Goal

In order to reinforce the power of the suggestion you are giving your subconscious through this visual aid and worded suggestion for your goal, and in order to make this key word or letter more effective so you are actually able to control your thinking, you must spend time studying your picture and reading aloud your worded suggestion. I recommend that you do this no less than 15 minutes each and every day. In a very few weeks you will be amazed at how well your key word or letter will affect your thinking.

Spend at least 15 minutes each day—and more time if possible. During this time, look at your picture and study it. When you read aloud that part of your written suggestion that states, "This Continental is mine," look at the picture and study the car in the picture, the color, the make, the model, the accessories on it. Visualize the car in your mind. When you read, "I already own it. It is mine now," again look at the picture and see the car parked in your driveway or you sitting in the car, whichever way you have composed your picture. Visualize yourself sitting in the car, driving it, parking it in the driveway.

A Reminder

Always keep in mind that you use only *creative* imagination and *creative* wording. Your thinking, your pictures, your words, and your actions, always show that the goal is yours already, you have it now. And always use as exact and vivid detail as possible.

Control Adverse Thinking

This key letter or word continues to be the symbol for your immediate goal until you have achieved it. And through use of this key letter or word you not only can reinforce the power of these tools and hasten the accomplishment of your goal, but you can also change or control any adverse thinking that comes into your mind.

If some obstacle crops up in achieving your goal or if some

occasional doubt pops into your mind that you might not be able to realize your goal, immediately use your key word or letter over and over again until you are thinking once again that your goal is yours. And remember that speaking the key word or letter aloud is more effective than just thinking it.

Use Repetition

After you have studied your picture and read your written suggestion and the summarization for your key word or letter aloud for at least 25 days, your subconscious should react to this key word or letter alone, even when you are not looking at your picture or reading your written suggestion. Continue to study your picture and read your suggestion aloud daily, but at any time during the day you may think, hear, speak, or see your key word or letter and reinforce this suggestion to your subconscious. Everytime you have an adverse thought about your goal, use your key word or letter again and again by merely thinking, speaking or seeing it.

Use your key word or letter repeatedly each and every day. Soon you will feel the power within you to accomplish your goals. Soon you will believe that you can achieve it. And soon it is yours. These key words or letters that you use actually cause you to feel it and believe it. And they cause your subconscious to react and materialize it for you.

Use Your Lines of Communication

Don't overlook using your worded suggestion and key word or letter during relaxation-concentration or when you are in self-hypnosis. Think your key word or letter to yourself whenever you use relaxation-concentration or self-hypnosis. Remember that communication with your subconscious is greatly improved at those times and you can convey this suggestion to him more effectively.

Examples of Other Goals

I have given you just a couple of examples of goals. Perhaps for health reasons you may wish to choose something on the physical side as your goal. Perhaps you would like more social poise. There are any number of goals which you might choose.

As I have said before, you should start with a minor goal at first, something just a little above what you have been able to accomplish in the past, until you become more adept and more confident in your use of these tools. Be realistic at first and practice using these tools. Prove to yourself the power of the tools so you may achieve increasingly greater successes. Develop a habit of success in achieving your goals to replace the habit of failure which most people have developed.

You can use these tools to achieve any goal you may desire once you learn to use them properly. However, regardless of what your goal might be, every time you compose a picture or write a suggestion, everytime you use creative wording, creative imagination, or acting-image, it must be as though you already have it. It is already accomplished. It is already yours. It isn't something that you will get or even that you are going to try for. It's something you have RIGHT NOW.

Develop More Personable Relationships

You may have a desire to develop a more personable relationship with people. If this is the case, compose pictures of people in various situations: pictures of someone introducing another person to a group; somebody laughing in a friendly gathering; somebody enjoying popularity at a party; somebody holding the center of attention at a conference or meeting. Then cut out pictures of your own face and place them in the pictures as though *you* are the one whom everyone is centered around or the one who is holding everyone's interest.

Then prepare a worded suggestion that, "I like people. I enjoy people. People like me and enjoy me. I like to listen to people and people like to listen to me. I speak clearly and fluently. I am constantly relaxed. I am confident," and so forth. At the end of your worded suggestion, sum up both your pictures and your worded suggestion into a key word or letter as I showed you earlier. Your key word here could be something like "confidence" or "friends." You could choose a key letter such as "C" or "X" or any letter you wish to use. You can even use a number as your key, if you prefer. Whatever you choose as your key, it remains the symbol for that goal until the goal is achieved.

Recognize the Facts

Recognize that your subconscious cannot tell the difference between an experience imagined in vivid detail or one that is real. This is also true of the words you speak. Your subconscious cannot reason with your words. And when you imagine you have something, when you act as though you have it, and when you say, "I have it," then you discover that your physical self is doing things to get it.

Your subconscious cannot reason and therefore it acts upon anything that you direct it to act upon with your thoughts, words, or acting-image. Since it cannot reason it cannot tell fact from fiction or fiction from fact. In order to get your subconscious motivated to action or to materialize the things you really want, you have to be the master. You have to use creative imagination with you being the master and creating the mental thoughts and pictures. You have to use creative wording with you being the master and selecting the words. You have to use acting-image with you writing the script.

Don't Interfere

Never try to use these tools to control or influence other people. Never use your creative imagination to imagine someone else working on your goal for you or to imagine that you achieve your goal through somebody else's efforts. Never use creative wording to suggest that "John bought the Continental for me," or "Henry gave me my new job." Never say that your goals are fulfilled by other people or that you influence others to do things for you. Your goals are strictly what you can do.

Other people do contribute to your successes and the achievement of your goals through the guidance of a Universal Force or some plan placed into effect by the Universal Force. But you should not be concerned with creating help or motivating other people to work on your behalf. Any attempt on your part to do so would serve no purpose other than to interfere with the higher powers that are working in your best interest and to delay or even prevent the realization of your goals.

How to Achieve Family Harmony

Let me give you another aid to your future happiness with an illustration of how to create harmony in the family. You can acquire the habit of happiness only if you, yourself, do something about it. Begin at home with your own family.

Your first step is to eliminate from within yourself any temptation to enter into an argument of any kind. You can do this by learning with your own family, if you will follow this program:

1. Place a large chalk board in some area of your home where it is seen by every member of the family at least once a day.
2. Make a written agreement between everyone in the family. It is necessary that the agreement be in writing and be signed by every member. Make certain that everyone understands clearly that this is a binding agreement upon each and every one of them.
   The agreement should state the following:
   a. It is agreed that anything written on the chalk board cannot be discussed or mentioned in any way, except for young children.
   b. It is agreed that each family member will read what is written on the board each and every day and will initial the board to show that he has read it.

      c. One member of the family shall be assigned each week to erase the initials on the board at the end of each day. His duty is to erase the initials only, and he may erase nothing else from the board.

      d. When something is written on the board, only the person who wrote it can erase what he has written. No one else can ever erase what another person wrote on the board.

3. When the written agreement has been signed by everyone, post it beside the chalk board.

4. Anytime an argument begins, or if you or other members of the family find anything that disturbs you, write it on the board. Once something is written on the board, it cannot be mentioned or discussed in any way as per the agreement.

     Write down the little, irritating things, too, as these often lead to bigger problems. And remember: Only the person who writes something on the board can erase what he or she wrote.

Examine what happens in this situation. First of all, absolutely no one can argue about or discuss what is written on the board. However, since everyone must read and initial the board every day, they remain aware of the problem and their subconscious begins working on it without their even realizing it. The person writing the complaint on the board may see it in a different light once it is written down. And he, himself, is automatically doing things to correct the situation which prompted his complaint. But the main consideration is that an argument has been avoided and harmony has begun.

By consistently writing down all problems, and by consistently reading them over and over again, you and all members of the family begin to find ways to correct the situation without even being aware of what you are doing. Since there can be no argument or discussion about what is written down, no one can dwell on the problem itself and your minds are left free to discover solutions and put them into effect.

You can go even further if you wish by penalizing anyone who begins to talk about what is written on the board. The penalty might be that the guilty party must subject himself to a game decided on by other members of the family; or, if an adult, he must treat everyone to a movie or an ice cream soda.

At first you may find a lot of nonsense on the board, especially from the younger ones in the family. But when you abide by the rules and the terms of the agreement, this nonsense soon disappears and problems begin to be solved. Some members of the family may feel a little hurt because of something written down. This, too, will soon disappear, and everyone will find himself actually appreciating the board. Everyone will know when anyone in the family is hurt or offended or bothered in any way, and something can be done about it.

If you will use this aid to family harmony, you will find more understanding and more togetherness in your family than you have had before. You will find the family working together better as a unit, playing together more often and enjoying each other more. Use it and see the results for yourself.

How to Have a Better Vocabulary

Quite often people feel their vocabulary is inadequate and that this shortcoming reveals to the world their limited academic education. They frequently feel that poor vocabulary alone is a tremendous handicap to any self-improvement or social successes they may aspire to. And many of these people suffer under the misconception that a good vocabulary can be acquired only through schooling or extensive reading and study which they "just don't have the time for."

It is true that the standard procedure through which people develop their vocabulary is schooling and the reading of good literature. But there is always more than one way to accomplish something. And because words are our primary means of communicating our desires and needs and are our basic form of self-expression, I would like to give you an effective aid which anyone can use to improve his vocabulary with very little expenditure of time.

Place a dictionary on the dresser in your bedroom. Every

morning when you get out of bed simply open the dictionary at random to any page and, without looking at the book, place your finger anywhere on the page. Then wherever your finger is pointing, read that word and its definition. Read the word and the definition only two times. Then while showering or dressing, repeat the word and the definition twice more. Make no further effort to remember the word or use it during the day. Many people do find themselves using the word during the day and many times afterward, but it comes naturally and without effort.

By following this very simple procedure, at the end of a year you find yourself with a remarkably improved vocabulary. And to make that improvement required no effort and only a few odd moments each day which would otherwise have been wasted and lost forever.

Will you still say you don't have the time to improve your vocabulary? Of course not. Those 20 or 30 seconds each day which you spend to open the dictionary and read the one word and its definition would go by whether you used them to accomplish anything or not. You are simply taking advantage of them to improve yourself.

But will you do it and create a successful habit which increases your ability to communicate and express yourself and which contributes to your future successes? If you merely say, "That's a good idea. I'll try it," you are accomplishing nothing. "I'll try," is not creative wording and it creates nothing—not even motivation. Don't try: do it. Place a dictionary on the dresser in your bedroom and leave it there for this purpose and affirm to yourself and to your subconscious, "I read one new word and its definition each and every day."

Take Action or Accomplish Nothing

When you use the tools I have taught you, combined with these aids, in communicating with and mastering your subconscious, you cannot fail. Every success you desire in life is yours when you use them properly.

Knowledge, however, accomplishes nothing unless you put it

to use, unless you take some action. So don't say, "I'm going to use this knowledge," or "I will use it," or, "I'll try." Affirm to yourself, "I use this knowledge each and every day in every area of my life." And begin to use it now.

IMPORTANT POINTS TO RECALL

1. The application of willpower and determination is not an effective way to break old habits or form new ones.
2. The easiest way to break habits and create new ones is through using the four basic tools.
3. Visual aids, showing your goal in vivid detail as existing here and now, are extremely valuable in achieving your goals.
4. Key words and letters, when properly used, symbolize both the picture you have composed as a visual aid and the creatively worded written suggestion for your goal. They also help you control your thinking.
5. Your written suggestion for any goal should include restrictions and the exclusion of any harm, suffering, or loss of any kind to yourself or any other person in attaining your goal.
6. These restrictions and exclusions in no way interfere in achieving your goal.
7. A letter, a word, or a number may be used as a key to symbolize your goal.
8. You should study your visual aid and written suggestion for at least 15 minutes each day.
9. Once a key letter, word or number is assigned to a goal, it remains the symbol for that goal until it is achieved.
10. After you have studied your visual aid and written suggestion repeatedly, your key word or letter is effective every time you speak, hear, think, or see that particular word, letter, or number.
11. Use your worded suggestion and key word or letter during relaxation-concentration or when you are in self-hypnosis.

12. Start with a minor goal and practice using these tools so you can achieve increasingly greater successes. Develop a habit of success in achieving your goals.
13. Never try to use these tools to control or influence other people.
14. Knowledge alone will not create unless you put it to use.

CHAPTER ELEVEN

How to Improve Your Memory Recall

Is your memory less than perfect? Do you completely forget names, past learning, important facts and figures? Do you find your memory becoming less accurate or failing you more and more often?

I am quite confident your answer to all three questions was an unqualified "Yes." But that answer is incorrect. Your memory is perfect. Recorded in your memory is everything you have seen, heard, spoken, or read from the day you were born. And your memory never fades.

I can almost hear your protestations of disbelief. You are ready to recite instance after instance when your memory has caused you embarrassment over a forgotten name, frustration because of a forgotten appointment, anguish when your memory of past learning has failed you in a test, aggravation because you couldn't remember where you put some misplaced item; and you are still suffering the repercussions of a forgotten birthday or anniversary. But I must repeat: your memory is perfect.

You Have a Photographic Memory

Earlier when we talked about the duties and functions of

your subconscious you learned that your subconscious records everything you see, hear, smell, taste, and feel; every sense impression within your range of observation. And these impressions are stored permanently in your memory bank. They are never "forgotten" and they never fade. You have a photographic memory.

A Scientifically Proven Fact

The truth of this fact has been proven time and time again through the use of hypnosis and scientific experiments.

Recall the incident I described to you earlier where a person in deep hypnosis would require literally hours to relate just the details recorded by his subconscious during the trip to my office. These people were not even aware of having seen or heard many of these details, but they were perfectly—and permanently—recorded by the subconscious.

If you yourself were to visit my office, even though that visit consisted of merely walking through the door, glancing casually around the room, and your immediate departure, if you were later placed in deep hypnosis you could describe my office and its contents to the last minute detail. Under hypnosis you would be able to describe the color, material and design of every piece of furniture or equipment. You could describe the pictures and certificates on the wall and recite verbatim the wording of the certificates. You could recall every title of every book on my bookshelves.

Your Personal Recorder

To begin to understand how this is possible, you must first realize that your subconscious records every sense impression regardless of whether you *consciously* observe that impression. You see—and your subconscious records—infinitely more things than you are consciously aware of seeing. You hear—and your subconscious records—infinitely more sounds than you are consciously aware of hearing.

Have you ever looked up a phone number in the directory and then had to look it up again before you could finish dialing the number? Your subconscious recorded the number the first time—and even many more names and numbers your eyes saw when you looked at the directory. But you did not have your conscious mind concentrated on the number and you did not consciously recall it.

Have you ever glanced at your watch to check the time and then immediately had to look at it again because what you saw did not register on your conscious mind the first time you looked at the watch? It registered on your subconscious the first time and was recorded by it, regardless of how inattentive your conscious mind may have been.

How many hundreds of times have you opened the medicine cabinet in the bathroom while shaving or brushing your teeth or going through your morning routine? Can you now consciously describe the contents on even one shelf of that cabinet? Probably not, because you never pay that much attention to it consciously. But your subconscious has recorded in its memory bank the size, shape, location and contents of every single item in the cabinet, including a verbatim record of the wording of each and every label.

Increase Your Awareness

So the first thing you must realize before you can understand this perfect memory, this photographic memory you have, and learn to use it more fully, is that your subconscious records everything you see, hear, taste, touch, or smell, regardless of your conscious observance or awareness. And the first step you must take in improving your memory recall is to become more observant, to become more consciously aware of things.

Recalling Names

When you are introduced to someone for the first time,

register the name in your conscious mind by addressing him by name during the conversation. If you do not hear the name clearly the first time, ask that it be repeated. If you have difficulty pronouncing the name, ask him to correct your pronunciation. Rather than being offended, he will be appreciative of your consideration and the fact that you are interested enough in him as an individual to be concerned about speaking his name properly. Once you have made it a point to be consciously aware of the name, then make no further effort to *try* to remember it. Know that the name has been permanently recorded by your subconscious and that the name is available to you whenever you wish to recall it.

Memory Recall

You will notice a few moments ago I said, "The first step you must take in improving your memory RECALL . . ." What people frequently refer to as a poor memory is, in fact, poor recall. You remember everything. But the portion of those memories you recall depends largely upon how your subconscious has been conditioned.

The second step you have to take in using this photographic memory you have to greater advantage is to recondition your subconscious to make its stored information available to your conscious mind. What you think of as poor memory is really only your inability to bring information from your memory storehouse into your conscious mind at will.

YOU CREATE Poor Recall

What I am about to say may be rather disturbing to you; but your subconscious has been conditioned not to make this information available to you; and you yourself have contributed greatly to this harmful conditioning. Consider the following statements very carefully. Which of these statements have you used, and how frequently have you used them?

I have forgotten.

I can't remember.

I can never remember names.

I can never remember numbers.

If you don't remind me, I'll forget.

I have to write it down or I'll forget.

My memory is very poor.

My memory gets worse every day.

I don't know where I put it.

I'll never be able to remember all of that.

I can't remember that far back.

That was too long ago to remember.

My memory isn't too good anymore.

I'd better tie a string around my finger or I'll forget.

I don't remember when.

I don't remember where.

I don't remember how.

I don't remember who.

I don't remember why.

Creative Wording

You have learned about creative wording and its power to create. You know that creative wording is accepted by your subconscious as an instruction when it is used repeatedly. What suggestion do the above statements convey to your subconscious? What do these statements create?

They instruct your subconscious to bury memories, not to make them available to your conscious mind. *They create poor memory recall.*

Acting-Image

Our very actions and thoughts are also instrumental in burying or minimizing our memory recall. We write reminder notes to ourselves; we make lists; we keep appointment books; we tie strings around our fingers; we even rely on a calendar to remind us what day it is. And these acts all imply doubt as to our ability to recall.

Creative Imagination

Through our creative imagination we create fear of poor memory recall. We are afraid we will forget a name and suffer embarrassment. We fear we will forget past learning and fail a test. We fear we will forget an appointment. We fear we will forget a speech we have prepared. And as you know, fear is very powerful in creating that which is feared. Again we are creating our own poor memory recall.

Power of Suggestion

Other people make contributions to your poor recall also. When someone asks you, "Can you remember . . .?" or "Do you remember . . .?" he is implying or suggesting that you cannot recall.

The very fact that we are given tests of past learning implies doubt as to our ability to recall. Many times, of course, tests are given to make certain the material has been studied. But most often they are given to review past learning, the implication being that our memories are not perfect and the material may have been forgotten.

From the time you were a small child you have received suggestions implying doubt in your ability to recall. Even as an infant you heard, and your subconscious recorded, statements to the effect that people forget, people can't remember, people don't recall, people become senile and their memories fade. You accepted these statements as fact and you believed that no one, including yourself, has a perfect memory.

This belief was strengthened by the admonitions of your elders to "Try to remember," or "Now, don't forget." And you have continually reinforced this false belief and buried recall through your own words and thoughts. Frequently you even act the part of someone who can't recall.

But you do have a perfect memory, a photographic memory. And your memories do not fade. With proper recall, those memories recalled to your conscious mind are as vivid as when they were first recorded.

A Contribution to Success

I'm sure I do not have to dwell on the benefits of improving your recall. I think the advantages of recalling past learning, or anything once read, once seen, or once heard being available to you at will for the rest of your life, are obvious to everyone. What a remarkable contribution such an ability would make to your future successes.

Begin Right Now

And right now is the perfect time to begin improving your recall by becoming more consciously observant and by reconditioning your subconscious to open this memory storehouse and make this tremendous wealth of knowledge available to you. As with all the tools you have learned of in past chapters, there is no great effort required in improving your memory recall. And as with all the other knowledge you have gained, this new knowledge does not create better recall unless you put the knowledge to use.

Believe in Your Perfect Memory

First, you must believe in your perfect memory, and know that your subconscious does record every impression from your five senses. You should know that when your subconscious is properly conditioned, he always makes this stored information available to your conscious mind at will.

Begin a Reconditioning Process

Second, you must begin to recondition your subconscious by

eliminating harmful creative wording which you have used in the past and replacing it with words which create what you desire: perfect memory recall. Replace the detrimental statements I listed for you earlier—and any others you find yourself using which limit your recall—with statements such as: "I know it, it comes to me." "I recall everything as I need it." "I have a perfect memory, and all its stored information is available to me at will."

Eliminate Fear

Third, eliminate fear of poor memory recall from your thoughts. Use the power of creative imagination to imagine yourself as remembering every word of that speech, everyone's name at the party, every bit of material covered by the test. Hold the thought that you do have perfect memory and perfect recall.

Act the Part

Fourth, create an acting-image of someone who recalls everything. It is not necessary to write a script to act this part. But when you make an appointment, make certain that you have the proper information clearly in mind, and then know that you can recall the appointment without the necessity of writing it in a book. When you go to the store, be sure to have the items you need firmly in mind, and then know you can recall them without a shopping list. Remove the habit of writing little reminder notes and tying strings around your finger. Know that you have a photographic memory and can recall anything and everything you desire to recall.

Keep the Line of Communication Open

Fifth, keep the line of communication open between your conscious mind and your subconscious so information can be received from his memory storehouse. If your boss were to approach you and ask, "Did you finish that report, did you finish that report, did you finish that report, did you finish that report?" you not only would have great difficulty answering, but I think you would also become a little irritated. And if he did this frequently, I believe you would soon find yourself taking considerable pains to avoid him.

But this is the exact predicament in which you place your subconscious when you repeatedly ask, "Darn it, what is his name, what is his name, what is his name?" If you continually repeat the question, you can't receive an answer.

It Comes to Me

Whenever you wish to recall something, simply say, "I know it, it comes to me," and then continue on with your conversation or activities and give your subconscious an opportunity to transmit the information you need to you.

It is not even necessary to make your desire for better memory recall an established goal to work towards. Your belief in your perfect memory and your constant awareness of proper suggestions to give him through your creative wording, creative imagination and your acting-image are sufficient to make astonishing improvements in your ability to recall.

Make use of this remarkable asset, this photographic memory you have, in creating more self-confidence, increased happiness, and greater successes in your future.

IMPORTANT POINTS TO RECALL

1. You have a photographic memory, as has been proven through hypnosis and scientific experiments.
2. Your subconscious has a permanent record, and a perfect memory, of everything you have seen, heard, tasted, touched, or smelled from the day you were born.
3. Your senses receive, and your subconscious records, infinitely more impressions than you are ever consciously aware of.

4. What is frequently referred to as a poor memory is, in fact, poor recall.

5. Your ability to recall has been diminished by past conditioning.

6. Memories do not fade. With proper recall, when memories are brought to your conscious mind they are as vivid as when first recorded.

7. Your ability to recall is strengthened by belief in your perfect memory and the proper use of the four basic tools.

8. You have to keep the line of communication open so information can be transmitted by the subconscious from its memory storehouse to your conscious mind.

9. Whenever you wish to recall a memory, affirm to yourself, "I know it, it comes to me."

CHAPTER TWELVE

Your Success Foundation

The tools for creating success have now been made available to you through your new knowledge of their existence and their limitless power. You have learned how to "sharpen" these tools and how to use them properly in building a future full of happiness and successful accomplishments.

Another Vital Element

But there is another very vital element, the single most-important factor, which must be considered always before true success and happiness can be attained.

This foundation upon which all successes must be based is people and your relationship to them. Other people are the building blocks which form the "house" within which you live your life. Your relationship with these people is the mortar which holds the building blocks together and determines whether the "house" you build with the tools you have available to you will be a hovel or a castle.

Look at It This Way

Stop for a moment and imagine yourself as the only living

man or woman on earth. If you were the only living human being, what would be of importance or of concern to you? Would not your perspective be altered? How drastic would be the change in your personal interpretation of "success"? What single factor to which you now assign such significance would retain its eminent position in your thinking if it were not viewed in the light of your relationship to other people? Material possessions, money, social position, professional achievements would all become meaningless if their quantitative value could not be compared to that held by someone else.

There are many people today who deny the importance of other people in their own life. Those of us who give consideration to our relationship to other people in our dress, our speech, our observance of prevailing social, civil and moral codes, are labeled individually as "squares," "conformists," and other derisive epithets; or we are lumped as a whole into the all-inclusive phrase, "the establishment."

But the truth is that other people are of paramount importance; and to be completely successful as an individual you must have a successful association with other people. A successful person accepts himself and does not necessarily look to others for approval; but he does conduct himself in such a manner that he maintains a rapport with his contemporaries and commands their respect.

Magical Ingredients

Following are some of the most magical ingredients of this mortar that becomes the bond of friendship and cements the human relationships in whose framework we must live our lives and create our successes.

Consideration

The most important ingredient in this mortar is consideration for other people. Be considerate of the needs, beliefs, and desires of others. Be thoughtful of their time. Do nothing that would detract from their pride or their dignity. You can never be completely successful as a whole person until you learn to be considerate of every person with whom you come in contact.

"I am always considerate of others."

Appearance

Enjoying a successful relationship with people does not necessitate the denial of your own principles or the circumvention of your own goals. When you are true to yourself, then you are true to those people who comprise the sphere within which your successes are to be realized.

Therefore, if you wish to be a "flower child," then dress accordingly. However, if your goal is to become a successful businessman, then dress appropriately to create an acting-image of a successful businessman and to evoke the approval and respect of those people with whom you must maintain a successful relationship to achieve that goal.

Regardless of your professional or occupational ambitions, if you wish to have a propitious relationship with people with whom you come in contact you must present yourself to them in a manner that is neither offensive nor objectionable to them. You must observe the fundamental rules of cleanliness, good grooming, and appropriate dress.

Too often our concern for these fundamental requirements of success are buried under a landslide of more conspicuous considerations. The subtlety of the contribution which immaculate cleanliness, good grooming and proper attire offer to your success remains subtle only so long as you are attentive to them. But there is nothing subtle about the contribution which lack of them—unkempt hair, offensive breath and body odor, dirty fingernails, soiled and inappropriate clothing—makes to your failure.

"I am clean, well-groomed, and appropriately dressed at all times."

Trust

You have to learn to trust other people if you are to deal with them successfully. In this vein I can neither add to nor enhance Emerson's perception of human nature when he said, "Trust men and they will be true to you. Treat them greatly and they will prove themselves great."

Moderate Praise

Do not hesitate to praise other people moderately when you can do so with sincerity.

Dr. Paul P. Parker's book, *How to Use Tact and Skill in Handling People* (copyright 1959 by Paul P. Parker, published by Frederick Fell, Inc., New York) related a study of school children and their reactions to praise as opposed to criticism and fault finding. "Fifty children were selected to study and recite arithmetic in one wing of the school and another fifty to study and recite arithmetic in another wing of the school. The teachers in the left wing of the school, in listening to the children recite and going over their arithmetic problems, very carefully showed the students the errors they were making. They aided the children in correcting the mistakes they had pointed out. In this wing, during the test period, the children had improved in their arithmetic 20 percent. In the right wing of the school the teachers proceeded on the basis of overlooking all errors. They encouraged the students by praising them for the sums they had worked out correctly. In this wing the students improved 70 percent."

The experiment proves that abilities wither under fault-finding but blossom under encouragement. This lesson should prove of value to you in your dealings with people who come under your influence or guidance. Place more emphasis on praising that which is praiseworthy and less emphasis on criticizing their imperfections, and you will be more successful in your relationship with them.

This is also excellent counsel to keep with yourself. Take a critical look at your own shortcomings; but then do not continue to berate yourself with further self-criticism. Praise yourself for your accomplishments and encourage yourself to greater accomplishments in the future. Begin trusting *yourself* and you will find yourself to be trustworthy. Treat *yourself* greatly and you will prove yourself great.

"I neither criticize or condemn other people."

"I praise all that is praiseworthy."

Be a True Friend

Before you can be a true friend to others, you must learn to be a friend to yourself. If you downgrade yourself, you can still admire and respect other people, but your admiration and respect will be offered grudgingly and tainted with envy. Similarly, if you do not believe in yourself and like yourself, you find it difficult to believe fully in other people and like other people.

"I like people and people like me."

"I enjoy other people, and other people enjoy me."

"I am a true friend to myself and to others."

Individuality

Accept other people as they are. Each person is different. Don't try to force people to conform to a mold designed by your own preconceived ideas. Treat each person as the individual he is and respect him for his individuality.

"I am always open to new ideas."

"I listen with an open mind to the viewpoints of other people."

"I learn from people."

"I discover the good in everyone."

Sincerity

Be sincere with people. Insincerity may escape detection temporarily, but it is always recognized in time. And once revealed, insincerity is the sure destroyer of trust, belief, and respect.

"I take a sincere interest in other people."
"I am always honest and sincere with other people."

Gossip

Gossip is such a despicable waste of words and time that I make no comment other than to state that gossip has no place in the thoughts or conversation of the successful person. It is just as harmful to the gossiper as it is to the person being gossiped about.

"I never waste my time, energy, thoughts, or words, on gossip."

Punctuality

Many unkind things may be said about the person who is not punctual. He lacks consideration, dependability and truthfulness; and a shortage of these qualities is a deterrent to any success.

"I keep my appointments."
"I am always punctual."

Spontaneity

Be more spontaneous with other people. Express yourself naturally and enthusiastically. Too many people feel that pure, heart-felt laughter, exuberance and enthusiasm are undignified. But a whole person is free to express his true feelings openly and honestly. He is neither reluctant to express honest indignation, nor embarrassed to show joy, love, and enthusiasm.

"I am spontaneous in expressing myself and my feelings."
"I am myself, and no one else."
"I am unafraid to voice my opinions freely."

Helpfulness

Don't be afraid to take time out from your own interests to help others. Remember that people are the building blocks in your own success. Help given to others without thought for material reward or gain often may be part of a master plan which has been implemented by a higher source for your own successes.

"I help others in every way I can."
"I offer assistance and guidance to others without thought for material reward or gain."

Prejudice

Our true life is spiritual; and as spiritual beings there are no discriminations as to race, color, or creed. Our physical bodies are merely the habitations for our spirits; and the color of that body in which a spirit dwells is no more a measure for judging the spirit than the color of the house in which our body resides is a measure for judging the man.

Other people contribute to your successes in life through the guidance of the Universal Force or some master plan put into effect by this higher power. In devising and accomplishing this plan, a Universal Force would neither recognize nor be influenced by such superficial considerations as race, color, or creed. Therefore, if you are influenced by such prejudices, you may well be interfering with, or even defeating your own successes. Prejudice as to race, color, or creed should find no home in the heart of any man.

"I neither judge nor discriminate against anyone on the basis of race, color, or creed."

Additional Affirmations

Following are some additional affirmations in the form of creative wording which you may use to develop more successful relationships with other people.

"I am confident."
"I enjoy the company of other people."
"I am grateful for each new opportunity to meet people."
"Every human being is important, and I treat him with the importance he deserves."
"I express my viewpoint and discuss matters freely, but I do not argue."
"I speak clearly to others and I make certain they can hear me well."
"I greet people warmly and enthusiastically."

The Importance of Other People

Do not underestimate the importance of other people to your own happiness and success. They truly are the building blocks for the framework within which you live your life. If you use every basic tool and exercise every power to the fullest but fail to recognize that the very framework of your life is comprised of other people, it is like accumulating beautiful treasures, priceless antiques, and overlooking the necessity of a house to put them in.

The Final Lesson

You now know who you are and how and why you became that person. You know that a successful life is founded in your relationships with other people. You have learned of these tools through which you can become the person you want to be and create every success you desire. You have been taught HOW to use these tools, and many aids in using them have been presented to you. And you realize that help is always available to you in any undertaking through a Universal Force which has supreme intelligence and knowledge. The time will come when you will be able to use these tools and powers to produce any right thing you might desire.

There is only one more lesson to be learned to complete your blueprint for success. It is a lesson which contradicts many things you have been taught in the past, but the truth of it is beyond value in creating success. The lesson is short in its simplicity, but very long in its wisdom: *Take no further thought.*

Simple as this rule is, it can be very difficult to apply at first. You have been conditioned otherwise all your life by suggestions that anything worthwhile requires willpower, determination and applied effort, and these are the only means of achieving anything in life. But these suggestions were given without benefit of the knowledge of the true powers of life, and they are an assumption that man, in and of himself, has greater power and intelligence than this Universal Force which either is or has access to the power of God.

Your Pattern for Success

When you have a sincere desire and have made this your immediate goal to work towards, then follow this pattern:

1. Create an exact mental picture of your goal as existing here and now. From this mental picture, compose an actual picture in vivid detail to use as a visual aid.
2. Prepare a creatively worded, written suggestion for your goal, again expressing your goal as existing here and now. In this written suggestion include restrictions pertaining to this goal and exclusions regarding the manner in which it is achieved.

3. Summarize both the picture and the written suggestion with one key letter or key word as your symbol for this goal.

4. Study the picture you have composed and read your written suggestion aloud for at least 15 minutes each and every day. Carry a small card with you on which you have written your key word or key letter. Then as often as possible during the day, look at this card and *see* your key word or letter, *think* your key word or letter, and *speak* your key word or letter.

5. When applicable to any particular goal, create an acting-image by preparing a written script and acting the part of the person it is your goal to become.

6. Take no further thought. Know that a plan is being formulated and implemented by a higher power with intelligence, knowledge, and a power to create which exceeds a millionfold any conscious efforts you are capable of making. Do not occupy your mind with conscious efforts towards planning or devising ways to achieve your goal. Leave your conscious mind free to receive guidance from the Universal Force. Know that no effort you could possibly make can begin to compare with the force which is working on your behalf, and believe in the achievement of your goal by this higher power.

The Magic in Believing

Formulate your goal, convey this goal to your subconscious and the Universal Force by using the tools creative imagination, creative wording, acting-image, and repetition, as you have been shown. And then take no further thought for the accomplishment of your goal, but believe that it is being fulfilled by this higher force with its infinite intelligence, knowledge and power.

When you faithfully follow this guide for the achievement of your goals, regardless of what those goals might be, you cannot fail. This is the magic in believing: the "magic" of healing, the "magic" of walking on water, and the other miracles related in the Bible. This is the "magic" of walking on hot coals 1,328 degrees Fahrenheit without harm. This is the "magic" which enables men to move mountains. And this is the "magic" which creates success.

Other Voices—Other Views

Now the pattern for success is complete. You have the pattern, you have the tools, you have the power, and you have learned HOW to use them. Undoubtedly it will require further study of the pattern and more experience with these tools before you become a master builder of success, but your apprenticeship has begun.

In studying and applying your pattern for success, don't overlook the advantages to be gained from listening to the viewpoints of others. Discuss the knowledge you have gained with others who have read this book. Form a discussion group with friends, neighbors, fellow employees, or even your bridge club. Remember that many minds working together are more powerful than one mind alone. Perhaps you have difficulty applying a particular tool, but another person in your discussion group may have understood this point more clearly and can clarify it for you. One person in the group may have a problem with a goal, and you might be able to point out some thought he expresses or creative wording he uses which has created an obstacle to his goal.

And just as each success you achieve strengthens your belief in the tools and, therefore, your ability to use them, each goal accomplished by a member of your group reinforces your belief. We see ourselves reflected in a new light through the eyes of every person we meet. And the people in your group can help you see the real "you" that lies beneath any false beliefs you might have about your own abilities.

If you have a desire to meet new people, you might ask permission to post a small notice in the bookstores to the effect that you are interested in forming or joining such a discussion group and would welcome hearing from others with a similar interest. I would suggest, however, that more results are gained when the group is limited to a fairly small number which can meet informally on a regular basis in the homes of the members. And each meeting should be held in the home of a different member to avoid creating an inconvenience for anyone.

* * * * * *

You now have a complete pattern for building every success which represents happiness, contentment, professional achievement, or material gain for you. Study this pattern with an open mind, perfect your understanding of it, and apply it faithfully in every area of your life, and YOU ARE SUC-CESSFUL.